The 3rd Paradigm

The 3rd Paradigm

A Radical Shift to Greater Success

Ivan Misner, Ph.D.   Dawa Tarchin Phillips
Heidi Scott Giusto, Ph.D.

Entrepreneur Press

Entrepreneur Press, Publisher

Cover Design: Andrew Welyczko
Production and Composition: Alan Barnett Design

Library of Congress Cataloging-in-Publication Data

Names: Misner, Ivan R., 1956- author. | Phillips, Dawa Tarchin, author. |
    Giusto, Heidi Scott, author.
Title: The 3rd paradigm : a radical shift to greater success / by Ivan Misner, Ph.D.,
    Dawa Tarchin Phillips and Heidi Scott Giusto, Ph.D.
Other titles: Third paradigm
Description: Irvine, CA : Entrepreneur Press, [2023] | Includes index. |
    Summary: "Backed by original research involving more than 4,000 business
    professionals, the authors present the three paradigms of business, the
    five types of Co-Creation, and a four part step-by-step model that
    allows you to make the radical shift toward the 3rd Paradigm of
    Co-Creation-where all stakeholders play a meaningful part in greater
    success"—Provided by publisher.
Identifiers: LCCN 2023003425 | ISBN 9781642011470 (paperback) |
    ISBN 9781613084595 (epub)
Subjects: LCSH: Executives. | Success in business. | Stakeholder management. |
    Executives.
Classification: LCC HF5386 .M638 2021 | DDC 658.4/09—dc23
LC record available at https://lccn.loc.gov/2023003425

Table of Contents

Acknowledgments

Writing this book was a 3rd Paradigm undertaking—and an act of co-creation. We are grateful for the more than 4,200 business professionals who provided invaluable data by completing our survey, laying the foundation for this book. We couldn't have completed this project without the insights we gained from you. Thank you.

Thank you as well to the business leaders we interviewed and corresponded with, especially Jon Berghoff, Rinaldo Brutoco, and Jerome Conlon, for their time, generosity, and insights. We would also like to thank Frank De Raffele for his thought partnership, friendship, and conceptual contributions. And thank you to the team at *Entrepreneur* who helped take us over the finish line.

CHAPTER 1

The Three Paradigms

We live in an age of sweeping conflict, widespread skepticism, and intense anxiety. Contention feels pervasive. Balanced discourse is a thing of the past, and pundits constantly tell us what's wrong with society. People complain like it's an Olympic event, and gurus in the marketplace obsess over the massive problems they see in the world. Negativity seems to be the norm.

However, we believe there is hope. There is an answer, and it starts with focusing on the solutions. When people focus on problems, they become world-class experts on "the problem." When they focus on solutions, they can become world-class experts on "the solution." **We believe "the solution" to today's massive challenges lie within the 3rd Paradigm.**

As a reference point, a paradigm is a philosophical framework or discipline within which theories and laws are formulated. We believe we are entering the era of the 3rd Paradigm. Let us take you on a short journey through what we define as the three paradigms of the modern era before we talk more about the solution.

The 1st Paradigm

The 1st Paradigm is the era of competition. This paradigm was formulated within the framework of the laws of production by early pioneers of business thinking. Formal theories of management began to be developed in the late 1800s by experts like Frederick Taylor, Frank and Lillian Gilbreth, Max Weber, and others who focused on issues like workflow, economic efficiency, and labor productivity. This was the era of "scientific management," which was the beginning of business theory. Scientific management's focus on production led directly to the 1st Paradigm's emphasis on competition.

The 1st Paradigm was so focused on productivity and competition that it failed to account for the needs of the people in the workforce. Competition was about gaining something by defeating your rivals or establishing superiority over them. It meant having a winner and a loser. The impact this had on individuals was generally minimized—unless it had an impact on productivity.

Can you imagine living in this production-oriented, competitive model today? Sixty-hour workweeks would be the norm, there would be few—if any—breaks, you'd be expected to work during much of your current lunch time, safety regulations would be nonexistent, and children might be working right next to you in a factory. In most "developed" nations, that now seems inconceivable, but in the late 19th and early 20th centuries, it was common throughout the world. In those countries where employees are still required to work extreme hours, it can easily lead to burnout, stress, and dissatisfaction in the workplace.

You might even be working in an environment like this right now. Did you find yourself nodding your head when you read about routinely working 60-hour weeks, eating lunch quickly—or even at your desk—and feeling stressed and burned out? If so, your company might be stuck in the 1st Paradigm, so focused on "getting ahead" of the competition that workers like yourself are left behind. If so, know there is a better way to do business.

The 2nd Paradigm

The 2nd Paradigm is the era of cooperation. This paradigm evolved over time as people learned that a strictly production-oriented approach did not take into account the interaction of the people involved in the process. This era was about two or more people working together toward shared goals. The focus on acting together for a common purpose started to evolve in the 1960s. Around this time, MIT management professor Douglas McGregor published his groundbreaking book *The Human Side of Enterprise* (1960), which introduced the concepts of Theory X and Theory Y. His framework highlights the motivating role of job satisfaction and argues that people can do their work without constant direct supervision. McGregor insisted that people are one of the most valuable assets for driving organizational success and that success comes from people being highly engaged in the process, with management recognizing employee contributions. His theory further focused on the motivating role of job satisfaction for individuals in the workplace.

We may be puzzled by this because these ideas seem so obvious now, but they weren't at the start of the 2nd Paradigm. This was, in fact, revolutionary management thinking in its day.

Ivan

Warren Bennis was on my doctoral committee at the University of Southern California. In his time, Dr. Bennis was considered to be the world's leading expert on leadership and organizational development. Years after I received my degree, I had an opportunity to have dinner with Warren. I was a member of the Board of Trustees of the University of La Verne, and Warren had been brought in by the university to give a lecture. Over dinner, Warren mentioned to me that he was a protégé of Douglas McGregor's while at the MIT School of Management. While I was aware of that, I hadn't known what he told me next. He said that there were numerous bomb threats against McGregor and the school because of his radical ideas about the importance of job satisfaction and people within an organizational structure. The focus on people was heretical to many back then. What seems obvious today was truly cutting edge in the 1960s.

During the time of the 2nd Paradigm, management consultant Peter Drucker developed the MBO process (Management by Objective), whereby managers and employees could identify common goals, define their areas of responsibility, and determine measures to guide the contributions of each individual. These and other advancements led to forms of collaborative project management, which enabled teams of people to collaborate across departmental, corporate, and national boundaries to achieve organizational objectives.

Today's organizations are much more collaborative. Old command-and-control methods have largely been replaced by much more openness and transparency than during the 1st Paradigm. Cooperation focused on better communication and compromise.

The collaborative approach used in large companies has trickled down to small and medium-size businesses as well. In a 2012 study entitled "Punching Above Their Weight," published in the *Journal of Small Business and Enterprise Development,* it was found that the vast majority of small businesses (almost 78 percent) were very open to collaboration as a way of developing their operation.

While the collaborative model was a massive improvement from the strictly competitive, production-oriented model, it was still lacking the full potential that the human experience can bring. In the 1980s, John Naisbitt wrote in his groundbreaking book, Megatrends, that humanity is moving toward a "high-tech, high-touch" society, saying that the more technologically advanced we become, the more important it is to become highly connected to people. Advances in management theory and technology have been leading society toward the next paradigm. It's important to note, however, that the transition from one paradigm to another doesn't happen overnight. They emerge by evolving over time.

The 3rd Paradigm

The 3rd Paradigm is the era of co-creation. This concept begins where cooperation leaves off. **The difference between cooperation and co-creation is the difference between working together and creating**

together. You may collaborate on a project, but you co-create products and services. Co-creation is a significant step beyond cooperation. It is about bringing different parties together to actually produce, improve, or customize a product or service, based on a mutually desired outcome. We define co-creation as creating value through a joint effort, typically involving both internal and external stakeholders.

While some scholars recognized the theory of co-creation in the late 20th century, it was in the 21st century that the internet brought the concept to the forefront. Crowdsourcing has become a critical tool for engagement. Waze, the navigation app, used by millions of people is a good example of this concept. The widespread application of digital technology has made customer empowerment a must. Crowdsourcing products and services such as Waze, the crowdsourcing app used by millions of people, is an early example of co-creation.

The difference between cooperation and co-creation is the difference between working together and creating together.

Society is rapidly moving from a passive to a more participatory consumer culture. Co-creation plays a key role in this, since today's consumers want a say in creating new products and services or improving existing ones. In their 2000 article in the *Harvard Business Review,* "Co-opting Customer Competence," C.K. Prahalad and Venkatram Ramaswamy make the distinction that from approximately the year 2000 and beyond, customers transitioned from being a passive audience to being active players—becoming "co-creators as well as consumers of value." In this age of co-creation, consumers want to work together with their favorite brands to ensure that products and services are adapted to meet their needs. In addition, many want to make sure there is a social cause related to the brand. Organizations engage in co-creation because they wish to foster the buy-in of stakeholder interest and increase value through innovation.

People tend to genuinely care about what they create. Throughout this book, we will talk about many different companies that actively employ co-creation. We include interviews that we've done with people who have experience in the co-creative process. Most important, we will provide you with hard data on the main benefits and drawbacks to co-creation, based on a survey we conducted of more than 4,200 business-people from around the world.

Many of the strategies incorporated into this book are based on those survey responses. In addition, we have integrated our experience along with various interviews to create a greater awareness of the 3rd Paradigm, which we believe will open a window to a co-creative future. Later in this book, we will share the impressions that the thousands of survey respondents shared with us about their co-creative journey, both good and bad. Integrated throughout this book is a comprehensive model for co-creation that has the power to make a difference in every business.

Running throughout the book is a story, *based on a true experience*, about an organization that ended up using all three paradigms before it could successfully implement a companywide project. The lessons from this tale are strong, real-life examples of how to implement (and sometimes struggle to implement) the key elements of the co-creative process. The saga begins here:

THE STORY

Richard was the owner of a midsize international company that was growing. It was the early 2000s, and the organization was still managing much of its operations through a paper-based system. However, several franchises in the company had begun to develop their own online database systems. Richard strongly considered creating such a system himself, but after long deliberation, he decided to allow the franchises to set up their individual programs. He believed that by allowing the franchises to develop competing platforms, one would prove to clearly be the best. He thought that the "cream would rise to the top," and the best system would emerge as the obvious choice for him to adopt for the entire company.

He was wrong. Decidedly wrong.

Oh, there were a couple of very good platforms, but none of them did everything needed for every level of the organization. Worse yet, instead of cream rising to the top, enormous silos were being erected throughout the company. People started to market their own silos to all the franchisees, which created confusion and frustration for many—especially Richard.

By 2007, Richard had realized that by allowing the various systems to compete, he had created chaos throughout the company, and it was almost too late to fix unless he took drastic action quickly. His strategy of allowing the independent programs to develop was a mistake. Instead of one or two programs being the obvious choice, many different programs were competing for supremacy in the organization. **It was a perfect example of the "unintended consequences of a seemingly good idea."**

As the owner of the company, he needed to come up with a solution. His natural instinct was to stand tall and let everyone know he was going to address the problem and find a single solution that would work for the entire company. However, from experience, he knew that running a franchise organization was a little like herding cats: everyone wanted to go their own direction, and the resistance to this decision would be enormous.

Although Richard's natural leaning was to make decisions and move forward, he learned over the years that this would often lead to repercussions that were as bad or worse than just pulling the Band-Aid off and going in a different direction. Actually, he first learned this lesson when he was about 13 years old, he had learned a valuable lesson in this regard. He was running for student council, and his mother told him, "Son, I love you, but you are a bull in a china shop. You tend to just roll over people when you disagree with them, and that won't serve you well later in life. You need to learn how to work 'with' people, not 'over' people." She handed him a paperweight that said, **"Diplomacy is the art of letting someone else have your way."** She added, "This is about collaboration, not manipulation. It's about working together with people to find a common solution. It is about cooperating with people to help guide them into the direction that you believe is best. When you learn how to do this effectively, you will become a true leader."

It was time, once again, to listen to that advice. Rather than simply deciding what was best for the company, he had to get their buy-in. He needed to get the key players in a room so they could help develop the best solution for the entire organization.

He accepted that competition had failed, and failed miserably. It was time to try cooperation—to let people offer their input and assistance to create one platform that would work for everyone. So, that year, Richard announced at a conference that the organization truly needed to have one uniform platform worldwide. It was hailed as a BFO (Blinding Flash of the Obvious) by nearly everyone at the conference. Now the question was "Whose silo, we mean platform, was the lucky one that would be chosen by the organization?"

According to his technology advisors, Richard was still ahead of the curve before the entire organization would require an online platform. The main problem with the existing platforms was that people around the world had a passion for their regional interests, but they absolutely did not grasp the full complexities of a global operation.

In 2008, Richard formed an ad hoc task force of about 30 key stakeholders and leaders in the organization. He was particularly keen to include people who had developed their own platforms in the process.

He brought these key stakeholders to the corporate headquarters for a two-day summit, where he meticulously laid out the global challenges and presented the requirements for a good platform that could be applied uniformly across the company. Richard was committed to the concept but not to a specific platform. He knew where they had to go, but was less concerned about what vehicle was going to take them there. Consequently, he focused on first coming to an agreement on the need for one uniform platform and then talking about what that platform would be. He told the task force that this singular platform would allow for global uniformity in tracking and reporting data. It would also tie the organization into a branded system that would be recognizable and usable to all clients worldwide, along with laying the groundwork for consistent future training programs.

He set forth this vision and then nudged, prodded, explained, and pressed the group to do the right thing for the organization. On breaks, he held individual meetings with key players to review his vision and gain their support. By the end of a very long day, the entire group agreed that the company should go to one platform.

Now came the more difficult decision—what platform should the company choose? Unfortunately, the one Richard proposed was expensive, so that was not popular among the task force members. After a second day of heated discussions, they agreed to have Richard's technology consultants pick one platform to test extensively. The consultants then reviewed the top systems and chose the one they felt was best. It was reasonably priced, and both the technology team and the task force supported it as an alternative to the more expensive platform Richard had proposed.

Richard had achieved what was unimaginable just days earlier: He got full consensus on moving the entire organization to just one platform. He succeeded because he was able to demonstrate to his task force that they would all be better off working on the same system. To their immense credit, they were willing to abandon their own silos and go to a platform that would be used by everyone. Richard was proud of this group for having the broader vision that the company needed to grow.

The system that they chose went into extensive testing for several months and worked incredibly well. Those stakeholders using the platform liked it immensely, until about one-fourth of the organization's data had been input into the system. **At that point, it crashed and burned like the *Hindenburg*.** The platform could not handle the massive amounts of data coming in from various countries around the world. Richard was numb. What should they do now?

The story above is only the beginning of the journey that Richard had with his company. Their story continues in each of the following chapters.

Conclusion

Co-creation is about creating synergy. The higher you go in the paradigm, the more positive people feel about the results. As you will see in the following chapters, when the process is implemented well, it can lead to amazing results. But it isn't easy, and it won't work for all companies (and definitely not for all leaders). As we said at the beginning of the chapter, "We live in an age of sweeping conflict, widespread skepticism, and intense anxiety." Our world is constantly disrupted, which leads to fear. We believe, however, that **co-creation can be a beacon of hope in a sea of fear** and that co-creation is the vessel to navigate through that fear.

CHAPTER 2

Business Transformation, Adaptability, and the Five Types of Co-Creation

Depending on how you grew up or were educated, you may view the world of business from any of the aforementioned three paradigms. Business attracts people who love the freedom of doing what they believe is best; however, what is "best" has evolved over the years.

It can be difficult to compete against businesses that are more efficient, more tight-knit, better organized, more integrated, faster, closer to the customer, better at managing costs, and better at generating through-put from generous contributions provided by all their stakeholders—in other words, businesses that are leveraging the 3rd Paradigm. It makes their rivals seem like lumbering dinosaurs, focused more on surviving extinction than on preparing for what is to come.

As one proverb says, "If you want to go fast, go alone; if you want to go far, go together." You can choose in which paradigm to operate, and you should ask yourself if your choice fits the problem you are trying to solve and how you are trying to solve it.

The 3rd Paradigm of co-creation doesn't just represent a skilled survival strategy for legacy companies. It also represents an entirely different business model and way of thinking, relating, and acting in a world in which customers are smarter, more critical, and more engaged with the products they buy.

The daily news cycle is filled with stories about seismic shifts in the way we organize our lives: the impact of rapidly accelerating climate change, the fragile interdependence of global markets, the threat of pandemics, the rallying of social justice movements, and the tightening competition for resources. As a person in the 21st century, you must learn to think ahead and be prepared for continuous disruption. You must be able to adapt.

As the technology sector accelerates its development, we all must learn to live with the powerful breakthroughs it brings, from autonomous self-driving cars to the highly advanced automated self-checkouts at stores and airports. You will have to completely rethink and relearn how things are done many times during your lifetime.

If you have a family, you will need to stay aware to provide them with the right kind of support and education to be safe and thrive in the emerging world. In business, you need to be adaptive and intently agile to reinvent yourself and your business according to the changing times, market conditions, and the needs and wants of your customers. Innovation and transformation, far from being buzzwords, are the new normal; you need to learn, apply, and master their processes and embrace their blessings and discomforts.

The need to adapt is certainly not new. As business professor Leon C. Megginson stated in a speech more than half a century ago,

Change is the basic law of nature. But the changes wrought by the passage of time affect individuals and institutions in different ways. According to Darwin's *Origin of Species,* **it is not the most intellectual of the species that survives; it is not the strongest that survives; but the species that survives is the one that is able best to adapt and adjust to the changing environment in which it finds itself** [emphasis in original]. Applying this theoretical concept to us as individuals, we can state that the civilization that is able to survive is the one that is able to adapt to the changing physical, social, political, moral, and spiritual environment in which it finds itself.

Like civilizations, we believe businesses must adapt in order to survive and thrive.

Some thought leaders claim business has the moral imperative to adapt. In his groundbreaking book *The New Paradigm in Business,* Rinaldo Brutoco recognized the incredible challenges that the post–World War II mass consumption economy has created—and laid bare what's at stake: "[I]t would be literally suicidal to continue employing the same business model, as can clearly be discerned by the fact that our current application of that model is destroying the planet." Despite many hurdles, Brutoco sees business as the *only* viable solution to the challenges we face. He argues business has a responsibility to act: "[T]he ability of business to resolve these perilous challenges translates into a *responsibility* for businesspeople to act as trustees for human society."

The species that survives is the one that is able best to adapt and adjust to the changing environment in which it finds itself.

We will help you see and appreciate the presence of co-creation as it is already apparent in your life and business. This book will leave you with a clear picture of when, where, why, and how co-creation can be a valuable tool and paradigm for you to step into—if you want to be part of the important changes happening in the world of business.

One important aspect of this book revolves around the data we collected and analyzed from our recent survey of more than 4,200 business professionals from around the globe. The survey results, which we'll discuss in detail in the next chapter, underpin the recommendations we make throughout the book.

The professionals who took the survey listed "diversity of ideas" and "increased quality of creativity" as major benefits of co-creation. But what does that mean?

All humans are creators. This process of creation can be entirely unconscious, so they might not even be aware of what they are creating, whether it's beneficial or destructive. Or it can be conscious, and they are choosing to engage with the creation process the best way they can.

This book is for the latter group. It is for the person who is not sitting idly by watching the future being written without them, who is determined to help create the world to mirror some of their best thinking, who wants to shape the world in the image of their best intentions, skill, contributions, work, and service.

What distinguishes co-creation from other forms of creation is how you go about it. How do you think about generating value when you are in the process of creating something that can be shared or offered to the marketplace? Who is actually involved in creating value, who receives the value, and what is really *of* value? Once you have identified that, you can disrupt your usual way of doing things and generate true co-creation.

Getting all stakeholders involved is the starting point of co-creation.

THE STORY

Our story picks up after Richard had embraced the 2nd Paradigm, cooperation. Despite involving key stakeholders, his franchise business was still facing significant challenges, and the new platform crashed and burned before it ever truly took flight. Still adhering to a cooperative approach, Richard started over. You will see how his company continued to struggle.

After the platform crashed in testing, Richard went back to the drawing board. He developed a plan using one of the legacy platform's developers and decided to build a brand-new system from scratch. They believed that the new system would be less expensive than what was first proposed but would be stable enough to handle the needs of the entire company.

It took more than a year to finish programming the new platform, and everyone involved, including Richard, was exhausted. He and his team had worked with many stakeholders for almost two years (first with the legacy platform and then with the new one) to develop an online system to support his company. The team made sure to take input from many people throughout the organization and invested a substantial sum of money into its development. He worked with the project manager, who talked to various groups of users to develop the system. After they received feedback from many of the organizational stakeholders, the release was imminent.

When the development team was ready, the platform was released with great fanfare throughout the entire organization. The fanfare lasted about two minutes. Maybe less.

In the time it took to execute a few keystrokes on the platform, the complaints started to trickle in. The trickle quickly became a stream. The stream became a river, and the river became a flood. Richard had expected the system to have some bugs, but it turned out those bugs were more like goliath beetles. And not just a few, but a really large swarm of disturbed, angry beetles, and they were all out to get him and the team.

Richard's initial reaction to the intense pushback about the platform was surprise and frustration. He had asked for, and received, substantial input. Hundreds of pages of input and hours and hours of discussion. The team had communicated with many arms of the organization to make sure that they implemented a platform that would address all the issues that were described to them. How could it possibly have gone so wrong?

His second reaction was that they needed a plan to get everyone onboard. Something that would turn the tide of anger and frustration. They just needed to understand…but then reality set in. He knew his stakeholders would feel that a pep talk was too little, too late—and they were too angry. They had to do a full reset of the project. But what would that look like, and how could the team make this iteration work?

Richard spent several days doing a debrief with his team to get a better understanding of why his cooperative approach hadn't worked. One of his technology people told him that he had a nearly impossible task. Many people kept saying they could make it work as long as it was done the same way as their old legacy system. She added that he wasn't just taking on a software project—he was tackling differing corporate processes around the world. Producing an online platform is a massive undertaking, but when you add the need to get all the stakeholders to agree to the same organizational processes when they had been changing things (without Richard's approval), that added a multiplier effect to the dilemma. For a franchise company, this was not good, and he knew it. The combination of the bugs with the platform and the vocal group who weren't getting features that were in a legacy system they had used, was creating an insurmountable problem.

But probably the biggest problem was that feature creep got completely out of control. In trying to make everyone happy, the team ended up adding so many elements to the platform that necessary tasks weren't finished. The most vocal people got what they wanted, but that wasn't the best choice for the organization as a whole. One of the tech people said it felt like the way people wanted some things was more important than the opinions of the programmers. In addition, Richard had promised to try to include everything from the various silo systems in this platform, which was eating up time and resources. That notion had to be abandoned.

People have a tough time conceptualizing something that hasn't been created yet. People in the individual silos knew what they wanted, but they couldn't envision the needs of the entire organization because they only saw their piece of it.

Obviously, the process wasn't working. Something dramatic had to be done to change the hearts and minds of the stakeholders. But what?

To Go Far, Go Together

Companies are getting better at understanding that involving their stakeholders early on can be a game changer. Jason J., a business owner and survey participant, stated, "[T]o pinpoint the optimal integrations, our customer service team collaborated with our clients to gain their insight and valuable feedback. From the data collected, we were able to increase our servicing capability and, as a result, have enhanced our clients' experience." When you begin to implement co-creation, its differences and advantages become obvious.

Having spent a considerable amount of time reflecting on co-creation, we believe there are two very different and important ways contribution-driven professionals can create value. First, value can be created by one individual or one group *for* others; or second, value can be created *with* those others together. When you are engaged in creating value *together with others*, that is the process of *co-creation*.

According to research supervised by Hal Varian, Google's chief economist and emeritus professor at the School of Information at the University of California, Berkeley, co-creation transforms the customers' role with the company:

> The key building blocks of co-creation are dialogue, access, risk assessment, and transparency. Dialogue encourages knowledge sharing, and more importantly, a shared level of understanding between customer and company. The goal of customers is access to desirable experiences—not necessarily the traditional focus on the ownership of the product. Risk assessment assumes "that if consumers become co-creators of value with companies, then they will demand more information about potential risks of goods and services; but they may also bear more responsibility for dealing with those risks." The fourth building block is transparency, where company information becomes more accessible to the consumer, which is necessary to create trust between the two parties.

This underlines just how large a shift co-creation can demand in the way you relate to everyone involved in your business, and how it can take you out of your comfort zone. Keep in mind that co-creation can require you to radically rethink what you are willing to share with your customers. As you keep reading and familiarizing yourself with the framework we present here and the different concepts and methods of co-creation that already exist, think about how you can use these techniques to unlock value.

All these methods have one thing in common: **They aim to unleash the synergy, capacity, and creativity of all stakeholders to optimize**

the path to mutually desired outcomes. And as such, they bring us one step closer to the reality stated by the popular proverb we opened this chapter with: If you want to go fast, go alone. If you want to go far, go together.

Success in the new era, especially lasting success, will be based on our ability to develop these kinds of co-creative approaches and solutions. These solutions connect us with one another as individuals, and they connect us to our biggest fans and most valued customers. Ultimately these co-creative solutions have the power to bring the world closer and help us deal with the challenges of our times in intelligent and innovative ways. That's not to say that it is always easy, as many people in our survey found out. Here is one such example, from a person who spoke of a drawback to co-creation:

> In the early days, a few business coaches got together to develop a new product. It was like herding cats and never got off the ground. We realized that egos have to be left outside if true co-creation is to be successful. People don't understand the art of co-creation. We are currently designed to not co-create—that has to be unlearned before successful co-creation takes place. Being awake to our current paradigm supports good co-creation and we get all of the benefits.

Like everything else in life, co-creation has a learning curve. **Co-creation allows us as business leaders to see areas of our business that most people overlook.** This is because we are willing to look at the entire creative process and take inventory of everything and everyone involved. It is an exercise in inclusivity, challenging the old selfish way of thinking that what matters most is *what's in it for me,* and replacing it with a deep understanding of the significance of the entire ecosystem of our endeavors.

Through the lens of co-creation, we begin to see the world differently—not divided into "us" and "them," but as an integrated whole, pushing, prodding, and challenging itself to become better and of greater value to everyone.

Business as Usual

Let's look at how a co-creative process compares with the traditional business models of the 1st and 2nd Paradigms described in Chapter 1.

As we mentioned previously, in a traditional model of value creation, an individual or group of people creates value *for others* when doing business or generating profit. In business, that model is called being *company-centric*. A traditional company-centric view states that value is created *by* one person or group *for* another. This model has several underlying functions and mechanisms that deserve clarification:

- The consumer is generally outside the value creation chain. This means that the product or service is created *for* them but not actually *with* them. The consumer simply buys the product or service and enjoys the benefit from that. Other than voting with their pocketbook, they have no direct influence on the process.

- The company controls what, where, when, why, and how value is created and added into the value creation chain. Companies and their owners control the whole process from beginning to end.

- Value is created through a series of activities that are controlled entirely by the company until the point of purchase by the consumer. That means that all value creation happens before the consumer is introduced to or takes ownership of the product or service.

- There is one single point of value exchange with the consumer: when value is extracted from the consumer in the form of payment and returned to the company in exchange for its delivery of the product or service.

We are all familiar with that type of business and that process of value creation and exchange. Many businesses are still successfully following this model and don't want to change. However, it is easy to understand that if value creation and exchange is the goal, then multiplying the times, opportunities, and scale of value creation and exchange with customers and stakeholders isn't just smart business. It also offers a strong advantage over those businesses that are stuck with a single exchange of value along their value creation chain—the one at the point of purchase.

Let's take a moment to examine how this different model is already being deployed by innovative companies across many industries and sectors around the globe. That model is *co-creation*; it represents a shift into the 3rd Paradigm, and it happens all along the value creation chain. Internal and external stakeholders are involved before, during, and after the creation of an innovative product or service.

The Co-Creation Approach

Co-creation offers a radically different alternative to the first two paradigms of competition and cooperation. It recognizes that building trust between all stakeholders is the single greatest asset and source of value generation—much more important than a simple value exchange during the final stage of the purchase.

If trust can be maximized throughout the value chain ecosystem of creators and producers, customers, end consumers, and other stakeholders, then everyone can benefit to the greatest extent possible from the total value of all existing relationships, and all knowledge and skills that exist inside the ecosystem. What this means in practical terms is that throughout the process of creating products or services, all important stakeholders, consumers, and customers are invited to add value through their individual contributions. They can make the products or services their own and improve them by influencing what, where, when, why, and how greater value is created and injected into the process and the final result.

In this way, **it is not just one side creating value for the other and exchanging it for a price. Instead, all sides are co-creating value together** and finding an equitable way of benefiting from the process and its results.

This *consumer-centric* and *stakeholder-centric* method of co-creating value executes a few important processes very differently from traditional business models of the 1st and 2nd Paradigms:

- The customer, end consumer, or other stakeholder is an integral part of the entire system of value creation from start to finish.

- They can actually influence what, where, when, why, and how greater value is generated. Here are a couple of ways they can participate:
  - ▶ Submission/tinkering: Customers have the opportunity to submit ideas, but the company still controls what they do (or don't do) with those ideas.
  - ▶ Co-designing: Customers are given total freedom to suggest ideas and, through a "voting process," select the winning idea in conjunction with the company. This is a way to leverage both the company and its customer base to create a final product, service, or concept.
- They need not respect the usual industry boundaries while searching for new ways of adding greater value.
- Each one can personally improve value creation and extraction and help make every product or service better at all times.
- There are now multiple points of exchange during the business process where they can co-create value together. From helping to design the best products to helping brainstorm new solutions, these opportunities can influence the value created and exchanged exponentially.
- This process generates loyalty and enthusiasm for products, services, and brands beyond the norm, as they now have skin in the game all along the value chain.

The way businesses develop products and services and bring them to market is just one way in which co-creation can be used to disrupt the way "things are done." It is what we have chosen to focus on in this book. One of our survey participants spoke to their need to balance the innovation associated with co-creation and the need to remain focused on production:

> One thing we have to monitor is the amount of time an employee devotes to learning and innovation and making sure that translates into business value—either for us or our clients. It's a tough balance to foster creativity and innovation while maintaining

consistent throughput and efficiency. We have devoted specific time periods for "playing and testing" vs. "producing," so that we are intentional, but controlled in our approach.

There is always learning involved, and it can take time to wrap your head around co-creation. We do want to introduce you to a few major types and protocols for co-creation so you can apply them to your business as you see fit.

Five Types of Co-Creation

Co-creation is unlike earlier business models, the latter of which business professors C.K. Prahalad and Venkatram Ramaswamy compared to traditional theater in a 2000 *Harvard Business Review* article:

> Business competition used to be a lot like traditional theater: Onstage, the actors had clearly defined roles, and the customers paid for their tickets, sat back, and watched passively. In business, companies, distributors, and suppliers understood and adhered to their well-defined roles in a corporate relationship. Now the scene has changed, and business seems more like the experimental theater...; everyone and anyone can be part of the action.

This is part of what makes co-creation so attractive: It is always a joint process. The group of people working together on a solution and the involvement of other stakeholders determine the form of co-creation you can or want to engage in.

And like all frameworks, co-creation comes with its own set of limitations and challenges you should be aware of. The drawbacks mentioned most often in our survey are *personality conflicts* and *dealing with egos*— not unusual problems when there are multiple cooks in the kitchen.

The Board of Innovation, a global innovation firm, also points to six barriers that arise, particularly in B2B contexts: cost, time, resources, capacity, creativity, and fear of change. Co-creation has immense potential but also risks. Choosing the right type of co-creation for your business is a crucial step to mitigate challenges.

We highlight five types, or frameworks, of co-creation throughout this book. They can be likened to five different paths, which can all lead you to your destination. Which road you choose depends on which path you consider the most suitable for your journey. The concise co-creative process we then outline throughout the rest of the book can be applied to each of these five paths of co-creation and represents the actual vehicle in which you will travel on your chosen road.

Some types of co-creation are more popular and thus more familiar to the average person than others. Many types of co-creation happen in plain sight, but unless you are trained to perceive co-creation in action, it might look very similar to a traditional business model. In fact, it is radically different.

Here are the five types we highlight throughout this book:

1. *Think tank/brainstorm:* A group or company brings together a consortium of people, experts, suppliers, and/or partners to develop a new solution, product, or service. In some instances, this even results in customers handling part of the "production" (e.g., flat pack furniture that customers transport and assemble themselves, self-scanning systems in supermarkets, and self-serve ticket counters at airports).

2. *Crowdsource:* A large group of people (often volunteers) co-create (often for free) a product or service by using web-based co-creative tools. (e.g., Wikipedia, Kickstarter). This type of co-creation can lead to *increased quality of creativity,* which was also one of the benefits mentioned in our survey.

3. *Open source:* A group or company invites a large group of internal and external experts to tackle its innovation challenge or contribute to its data pool (e.g., Center for Open Science and ResearchGate). This can lead to what many participants in our survey described as a *shared sense of ownership and shared resources.*

4. *Mass customization:* A group or company mass-produces products that have been individually tailored to the customer's wishes.

(e.g., a T-shirt printed with your own photo, personalized Vans shoes, or customized luggage). Many participants in our survey mentioned the *diversity of ideas* as a major benefit of co-creation.

5. *User-generated content:* A group or company uses knowledge and content that is made public by people (e.g., posted online). There are all kinds of web tools to help you find very quickly information that others have posted online (e.g., customer feedback on blogs and forums, YouTube videos, and social media platforms). This is another great example of gaining *access to shared resources,* which many in our survey listed as one of the advantages of co-creation.

You can also group these five types of co-creation into just two different buckets:

1. According to what role the group or company plays in the process: This is about **who steers the process.** Is it the individual consumer, or the company?

2. According to the kind of value created: This is about whether your value is a **standardized value** that all customers can enjoy (co-creating a better product or service), or a **personalized value** individually tailored to each customer (co-creating a personalized product or service).

Co-creation, following the five types above, is about making something *better* or making something *unique.* If unique is the value proposition, even average products can find market success because they tap into the value of co-creation. If it is making something better, even average products can still find market success by being improved with the help of customers and consumers.

That is why co-creation is continuing to rise in popularity among new and established businesses alike. What type of co-creation would work for you and your company?

As you can see, co-creation can unlock additional value in your value creation chain and make that value available for your and others' success. Wouldn't it be great if you could optimize the value you provide because you trust and engage with others, rather than keeping your value generation tied to an outdated model? Wouldn't it be meaningful to elevate your relationships and engage the talents, knowledge, and skills of those who care the most about what you do—your customers and the consumers and stakeholders of your products and services?

There is no aspect of your business that cannot be touched and improved upon with the help of co-creation. Every part of every business can benefit from unlocking and harnessing the power of co-creation to identify the value yet to be discovered, unleashed, and scaled. Every business could achieve greater success by embracing the co-creative process and expanding the trust and investment it can generate among customers, consumers, and stakeholders alike.

We looked at each of the five types of co-creation to formulate a Co-Creation Model, which we will introduce in Chapter 4. Understanding how each of these types work will help position you to implement co-creation in your business. Consider these processes when creating a Co-Creation Model in your group or business.

Type One: Think Tank/Brainstorm

Human Interaction: Using a think tank or brainstorming is a familiar way of co-creating. In this approach, you are bringing together a group of people to help you generate new ideas or help innovate new products, services, systems, and processes. Here are some examples:

- Creating an unforgettable customer service experience that has never been seen before, in your industry or in general
- Generating new marketing ideas that are inexpensive but achieve greater prospect and customer engagement and drive more people to your door
- Reinventing sales processes that break the mold of your old sales results and help your customers self-sell and upsell
- Reimagining management processes that allow your people to focus less on running the systems and more on interacting and engaging with one another on a daily basis

- Mining for key leadership development and personal growth that allows your company to reach and maintain peak performance with less effort

- Creating a system where conference attendees choose at the conference what they want it to be about

Many well-known companies use this approach to co-creation.

- **Xerox Corporation**, for example, regularly looks for intersections between different ideas and how they might merge and give rise to completely new ideas. Each year, company funds are set aside to encourage and support employees to network and develop new ideas that otherwise wouldn't get off the ground.

- Starting with an end product in mind and brainstorming all the way backward until an idea emerges that combines cost considerations with technological necessities is how **McDonald's** innovation team generates new breakthroughs. Those ideas can then get prototyped and tested quickly, often in as little as a day.

- **Google** has developed a product called Workspace, an online collaboration tool that can help manage innovation processes by making it possible for people to directly work on shared documents. **Ideawake**, **Brightidea**, and **Mural** are other companies offering technology solutions to help with the brainstorming process.

To work as a creative and diverse team and achieve some actual co-creation, your think tank must have the right focus. Creativity and innovation will naturally happen when the right causes and conditions for co-creation exist. You achieve this by paying particular attention to who is in the room and how you set up the process, as you will see in Chapter 6.

Brainstorming can present challenges, just like other forms of co-creation. **The co-creative process can be rife with conflict.** In our survey, we have seen people aware of the pros and cons of the human interaction side of co-creation, especially when it comes to think tanks and brainstorming. Sometimes, the lack of clarity and division of tasks creates the challenges, as one survey respondent shared: "When everybody has an opinion, deadlines are rarely met, and several variations of the project are created—which is a waste of resources. Overlap of skill sets and roles is a big issue." That is when it is especially helpful to follow a proven process. Sometimes, it is how people communicate with each other that causes the issues: "The discussions went around and around and around and became a platform for ego touting rather than actual development of a product." Or people simply fail to be open and listen to what is being generated and presented during the process:

> We had one of our employees bring up an interesting concept, and before he was able to fully present his idea, the crowd took turns finding the reasons why this would not work. If this discussion was preplanned and given an opportunity to be thoroughly presented and feedback was solicited, then a more productive follow-up session could have addressed the "perceived" negatives.

These are not uncommon challenges, our survey found, but they can be overcome with a clear co-creative model and process.

Type Two: Crowdsource

Human Focus/Tech Hosted: One of the most powerful ways of co-creating is to *crowdsource*. Crowdsourcing refers to obtaining input or information from a large group of niche people or the general population via the internet.

Below are some crowdsourcing examples that probably sound familiar:

- **Waze:** Waze is a successful crowd-powered app that automatically generates the optimal route for a driver to take. Information is crowdsourced by users reporting road closures and other traffic incidents and by measuring drivers' speed to determine traffic jams.
- **IKEA:** Co-Create IKEA is a digital platform built by furniture retailer IKEA to gather ideas from customers and university students on new and innovative product solutions. Viable product

designs may be licensed or offered an investment by the company. The company is providing substantial financial incentive to the professional community if their ideas are selected for further development by IKEA, and countless ideas for new products or variations on existing ones have so far made it through Co-Create IKEA to the market.

- **Lego:** The company allows users to design new products and test the demand. Anyone can submit a design other users can vote for, the most popular ideas—such as musical instruments, famous artworks or spacecraft models—get moved to production, and their creators get paid one percent royalty on net revenue. Innovative product ideas and customer engagement have seen continued increase, and the buzz has been superior to any other method, as creators take it upon themselves to promote their ideas and, in doing so, promote the company.

As you can see, this type of co-creation happens through careful strategic planning and implementation, and with the input coming from the consumer group or desired target market.

Type Three: Open Source

Technology/Human Interaction: Open source is a technology-driven environment with high-tech users serving as the collaborators and innovators. Open source software, for example, is based on a structured platform, but the original source code is made freely available so it can be redistributed and modified.

In open source, technology is enhanced by the ongoing contribution of human innovation.

Here are some open source examples:

- **Linux:** The Linux family of operating systems is one of the most successful examples of open source software in the world. Linux's source code can be used, modified, and distributed commercially or noncommercially by anyone under the terms of its licenses. Today, about 90 percent of all cloud infrastructure and roughly 74 percent of all smartphones in the world are Linux-based.

- **Center for Open Science's Open Science Framework** is an open source web depository for scientific research. It allows scientists from around the world to get access to the work of other scientists and shorten the learning curve of research. It also allows for the many unpublished research studies conducted each year to publish their results transparently online so other scientists can discover additional results not generally available in the few popular peer-reviewed scientific journals.

- **VLC Media Player** is a free multimedia player used for video, media, and audio files. VLC Media Player plays discs, webcams, streams, and devices, as well as streaming podcasts. It offers a plethora of extensions and skins that allow you to create customized designs and runs on Android, Mac OS X, Linux, Windows, Ubuntu, and iOS.

Open source projects require an appreciation not only for the value we can create together but also for drastic innovation. Such innovation occurs by removing the limitations of competitive business models and the secretive mentalities around core processes.

Type Four: Mass Customization

Technology Developed/User Driven: Mass customization is a way for consumers to influence the design or product development process to receive more customized products or services. With mass customization, more people receive exactly what they want by directly co-creating it themselves.

This can be anything from a single feature to the entire product or service. Here are some examples of mass customization:

- **Nike:** Customers of the athletic wear and shoe manufacturer can upload their own designs to co-create a shoe that reflects their exact desires.

- **Vans** is another example of a shoe manufacturer that uses mass customization to co-create its products by allowing customers to choose colors and patterns, upload a custom picture, or click a "randomizer" to see what you get.

- **Teespring** is a clothing manufacturer that offers its customers design studios, where they can create their own T-shirt designs and then offer them for sale in their own online store or through social media.

- Car manufacturer **Tesla** allows its customers to select from a palette of offered features and benefits just like you would off a menu in a restaurant. And while all car manufacturers give you a certain amount of customization to choose from, Tesla stores seem more like design studios and less like car dealerships when you enter them. And the company has locations where customers can pick up the car they ordered online without ever having to set foot in a car dealership.

With mass customization, customers can express their unique personalities and preferences through skillfully developed platforms that capture market share by empowering their creative potential.

Type Five: User-Generated Content (UGC)

Technology Developed/User Contributed: User-generated content (UGC) is a system of co-creation by which users of a technology platform themselves create the content that is being offered through the platform. The age of social media has seen a steady increase in companies that use co-creation to increase their value. Some examples of these companies include:

- **YouTube** allows people to upload their own videos and create personal video channels. Today it is the second most visited site on the internet, with 720,000 hours of content uploaded each and every day, and nearly 30 billion hours of video viewed each month.

- Social media giant **Meta** (formerly Facebook) gives people their own profile to connect with friends, work colleagues, and other people they know to share pictures, music, videos, articles, and stories about their life and join other like-minded people in shared interest groups.

- People on **Instagram** can upload photos and videos and share them with their "followers" or with a select group of friends. They can also choose to view, comment on, and like posts shared by their friends on Instagram.

- **Pinterest functions as** a visual discovery engine to help people find new ideas to inspire them, such as recipes, home decor, or fashion. The platform lets them save those ideas to idea boards to keep them well-organized and easy to find.

- **Twitter** is designed to allow people around the world to communicate and stay connected through short messages, called *tweets*, which can contain photos, videos, links, and text. Tweets are posted to your Twitter profile, made available to your followers, and are searchable.

Customers post their own content on these platforms, and the companies make that content available to other users. Thus, user-created content reaches more and more people, attracting attention, which the companies then convert into advertising revenue through offering businesses the opportunity to market on their platforms.

Conclusion

These five different co-creation methods all work to generate great value and ROI in business regardless of the industry.

Yet there is a difference between knowing about something and actually doing it. This is sometimes referred to as the knowing-doing gap. And it is your job to cross this gap by getting into the game and starting to use some of these co-creation approaches yourself.

Visionaries and innovators around the world are applying these co-creation methods to new and old challenges. Solving problems for customers, consumers, and stakeholders, and doing so profitably, is not unique. What is unique is that with these methods they can unlock innumerable opportunities along the value creation chain where more value can be generated—and those are far beyond any one individual's ability to generate or create.

That is what makes co-creation an exciting proposition for you. It is also why we believe you can benefit from understanding, appreciating, and applying this 3rd Paradigm of business in your life as well.

CHAPTER 3

The Survey Says...

We have personally seen co-creation in action and have witnessed the powerful impact it can have in organizations. However, we felt it was important to anchor our opinions with hard data from business professionals around the world. Consequently, for more than a year, **we conducted a survey and gathered more than 4,200 responses from businesspeople** around the world.

We didn't want to *just* give you our viewpoint and those of other writers and experts. We wanted to share ideas and insights from people in the field who have had good and bad experiences with co-creation.

Based on other books we've worked on, we have found that survey results genuinely help when writing a book. They provide important signposts to follow and sometimes epiphanies that we had never previously considered. Some people are not comfortable with data, and we understand that. Our goal is to unpack the data in a way that gives context to critical concepts for building a co-creative organization. Co-creation is a valuable tool that business leaders can rely on again and again. As you'll see from our survey results, some organizations deploy co-creation on a project-by-project basis, while others operate co-creatively almost all the time.

This chapter provides an overview of summary data that we discovered during our research for this book. It also lays the foundation for the comparisons that come later as well as the next installment in Richard's continuing co-creation story, which we have told in previous chapters. In addition to the summary data, we've included information about the survey's respondents: gender, age, and the size of their organizations. This might give you a more nuanced look at the impact that co-creation can have within an organization.

Gender

Almost 53 percent of the respondents to our survey were men and 47 percent were women, showing a reasonable distribution based on gender (see Figure 3.1 below). Later in the book, we will look at what impact gender may have had on opinions related to co-creation.

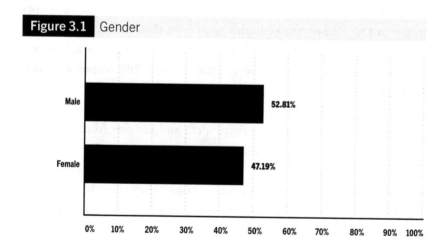

Figure 3.1 Gender

Age

We felt that age might be an important factor regarding co-creation, so we asked people to share their age in the survey (see Figure 3.2 below). At the time of the survey, the 29 and younger age bracket was represented by Gen Z and Millennials. The 30–39 age bracket were strictly Millennials. The age distribution of the respondents was skewed more heavily toward experienced professionals of at least 40 years of age. The

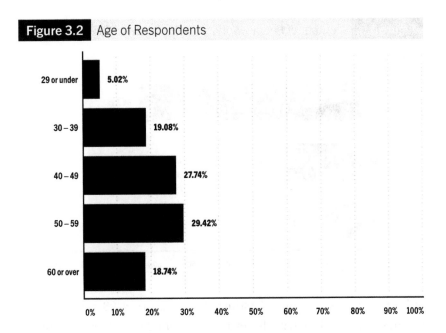

Figure 3.2 Age of Respondents

40–49 bracket was strictly Gen X, with the 50–59 group being a blend of Gen X and baby boomers. Finally, the 60 and above age bracket was represented predominantly by baby boomers.

Later in the book, we will look at what impact age may have had on opinions related to co-creation.

Size of the Organization

Another factor we felt would be important in reviewing the benefits and drawbacks of the co-creative process was the size of the individual's organization.

As you can see in Figure 3.3 below, almost 65 percent of the respondents were involved in companies with 10 or fewer employees, about 23 percent were involved in companies with 11 to 100 employees, and nearly 12 percent with companies having more than 100 employees.

While the survey seems to have a disproportionate number of respondents from companies with fewer than 100 employees, that is reasonably close to the overall percentage of businesses. The Small Business

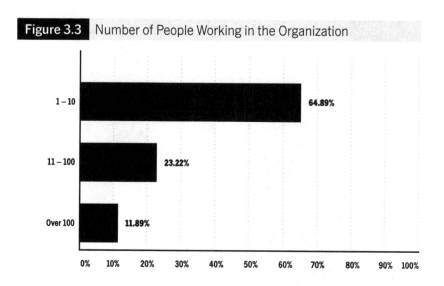

Figure 3.3 Number of People Working in the Organization

& Entrepreneurship Council estimates that just over 98 percent of all businesses in the U.S. have fewer than 100 employees (a similar number to many other countries). Our survey has roughly 88.1 percent of respondents with organizations of that size.

Later in the book, we will look at what impact the size of the organization may have had on opinions related to co-creation.

Top Seven Benefits of Co-Creation

Assessing the benefits of co-creation offers valuable information to leaders who seek to use the 3rd Paradigm effectively. Consequently, **a sizable portion of the book will be devoted to examining the benefits of co-creation,** as outlined by our survey respondents, interviews, and our own observations. We first conducted a pre-survey, asking hundreds of respondents what they felt were the key benefits and drawbacks of co-creation. From that, we compiled a list of roughly two dozen factors. Figure 3.4 below shows the top seven benefits of the co-creative process, as determined by the full survey. Because respondents could select more than one benefit relating to the process, the total percentage for all the benefits is well over 100 percent.

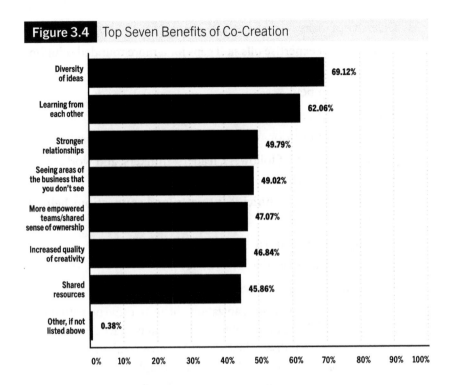

Figure 3.4 Top Seven Benefits of Co-Creation

The top seven benefits of co-creation, based on our survey of more than 4,200 respondents, were, from highest to lowest:

1. Diversity of ideas
2. Learning from each other
3. Stronger relationships
4. Seeing areas of the business that you don't see
5. More empowered teams/shared sense of ownership
6. Increased quality of creativity
7. Shared resources

In the survey, we asked the respondents if they would like to comment on various aspects of co-creation. We received almost 1,000 open-ended responses. Below are some representative observations from the survey respondents relating to each of the top seven benefits shown above and discussing why these factors added value to co-creation.

1. Diversity of ideas
   ▸ Diversity of expertise fills skill gaps for a more rounded solution.
   ▸ There is a diversity of ideas, even if people are not proven experts in a field.
   ▸ Best project results came from working across cultures.
   ▸ Diversity of positions resulted in good input to the project.
   ▸ A diverse group of followers, leaders, thinkers, and workers helped the project.
   ▸ **Diversity of age, ethnicity, interests, and connections helped greatly.**
2. Learning from each other
   ▸ Power of brainstorming
   ▸ Fresh ideas and new ways to look at problems
   ▸ At a large supermarket organization, the team came up with the simple idea of placing a rubber "stopper" on the racks that would keep the merchandise pulled forward to give a "full inventory" impression and established a minimum number for inventory before reorder. We were able to reduce the amount of inventory by 48 percent (millions of dollars) with no negative effect on sales.
3. Stronger relationships
   ▸ Synergies are created with the relationships that develop.
   ▸ The concept of using teams to create and innovate has resulted in significantly stronger buy-in and trust from the end user. When people know that the process for creation isn't a top-down approach, it leads to a powerful shift in culture toward the positive and growth for all involved!
   ▸ Significant involvement from others in my organization led to better relationships.
4. Seeing areas of the business that you don't see
   ▸ Team members were from different expertise areas; each of them were heavyweight experts, professional, used time efficiently without creating much of those negatives, and reached to innovation.

- **By looking at the problem from all angles, we were able to see the solution more clearly.**
- People discovered issues that they wouldn't otherwise see or understand.
- Thinking of things that I would not have seen from my perspective.
- Hearing things you would have never thought of

5. More empowered teams/shared sense of ownership
   - Vested interest in the outcome
   - Getting alignment of the team
   - The team approach created better services for the clients.
   - Getting the sales team, production team, and administrative team together created a stronger organizational team.

6. Increased quality of creativity
   - Too much to do, to do it all alone. It's difficult to be creative if you are overwhelmed with work.
   - We had a great collaborative project that won a contract to provide an innovative solution to a compliance issue through training and onsite coaching.

Why stand alone in front of a difficult decision when one can leverage their network? People working together definitely adds an increased level of creativity to the mix of opportunities.

   - We all are masters of our own industries, and this alliance can create a tremendous value for any big organization in achieving their goals.
   - **Why stand alone in front of a difficult decision when one can leverage their network?** People working together definitely adds an increased level of creativity to the mix of opportunities.
   - Creativity! People come with such differing ideas for ways to reach the same objective.

7. Shared resources
   ▸ Sharing knowledge with people with fewer resources is very valuable.
   ▸ Pooling various skills is vital to serve the clients.
   ▸ Shared resources free up time for other activities.
   ▸ It allows someone to see aspects of the operation from design to execution in ways that they didn't have before.
   ▸ Pooling individual strengths and expertise resulted in better results.
   ▸ Bringing additional resources to a project increases the client's confidence.

Top Seven Drawbacks to Co-Creation

While it is important to understand how to make co-creation work successfully, it is equally important to know what to sidestep when implementing a co-creative strategy. **Without knowing what problems to navigate and what to avoid, the best intentions can lead to disaster.**

The top seven drawbacks of the co-creative process, based on the survey, were, from highest to lowest (see Figure 3.5 below):

1. Personality conflicts
2. Dealing with egos
3. Poor communication
4. People who don't pull their weight
5. Lack of agreement on who makes the final decision
6. Individuals hijacking the direction of the project
7. Nonaligned vision for the project

Below are representative observations from the survey respondents relating to each of the main drawbacks of co-creation, culled from nearly 1,000 open-ended responses.

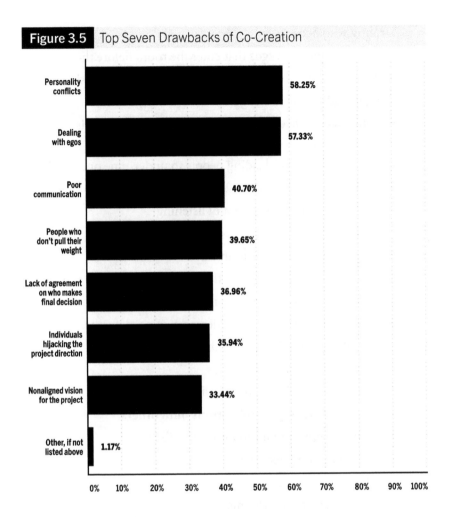

Figure 3.5 Top Seven Drawbacks of Co-Creation

1. Personality conflicts

   ► **Disputes based on personality differences slow the co-creative process.**

   ► Clashes occur between parties who normally don't get along.

   ► The loudest person tries to control the process.

   ► Different temperaments don't get along in the process.

   ► Competitiveness creates chaos in the process.

   ► People who disagree with a team member will sometimes undermine the direction of the entire project.

2. Dealing with egos
   - ► Some people have egos that enter the room before them.
   - ► Those with a superiority complex try to control decisions.
   - ► Egos lead to power struggles.
   - ► **Some people love to talk, and their favorite subject is themselves.**
   - ► Egos get in the way leading people to undermine one another.

3. Poor communication
   - ► A lot of talking but not a lot of listening
   - ► Lack of input
   - ► Progress not being communicated
   - ► No understanding of where the project stands in the process
   - ► No written outline of the project
   - ► Lack of dialogue due to the hierarchy of participants

4. People who don't pull their weight
   - ► Lack of attendance at meetings
   - ► People abdicated their responsibilities.
   - ► **Individuals dumped obligations onto others.**
   - ► Didn't get upfront buy-in for responsibilities
   - ► Some roles were neglected or rejected.
   - ► Subpar work from some

5. Lack of agreement on who makes the final decision
   - ► Too many people trying to be the leader
   - ► No leader resulted in difficulty reaching agreements.
   - ► Conflict between people trying to lead created a poor dynamic.
   - ► Too many cooks in the kitchen syndrome

6. Individuals hijacking the direction of the project
   - ► **Some individuals had ulterior motives.**
   - ► Some people didn't share information to benefit themselves.
   - ► Repeated interference in areas that were not in someone's area
   - ► People hijacked discussions to go in a different direction.

7. Nonaligned vision for the project

   ► Lack of a commonly agreed objective

   ► Discussions going in circles

   ► Endless discussions and disagreements without a clear vision

   ► A lot of discussion without a clear "end in mind"

   ► A lack of actionable, measurable plans

Later in the book, we will take a deeper dive into the data summarized here and unpack these findings by comparing and contrasting them with other important factors. In doing so, we will outline the "dos" and "don'ts" for a successful co-creative process within an organization. As part of this analysis, we have cross tabulated key factors mentioned above (age, gender, size of organization) as they relate to the impressions people have of the positive and negative elements of the process.

Most important, we discuss this data as it applies to the Co-Creation Model that is a cornerstone of our concept when it comes to implementing it in your organization. **The data helps us examine a subjective process in a more objective way.** By knowing which strategies have worked well for other organizations, as well as which major hurdles people have encountered, it allows us to be more successful in our pursuit of co-creation.

THE STORY

We'll conclude this chapter by taking you back to Richard's story. He lacked all the data we—and now you—have about the concept of co-creation, or its benefits and challenges. Like many business professionals, his efforts to fix an issue were well-intentioned but a little like walking through a maze blindfolded. It took him a long time and a lot of money to work out a successful co-creative strategy.

Richard had now decided what he needed to do: reset the entire project! Ugh. They had already spent hundreds of thousands of dollars on the program, and most of it had to be tossed. There was no way he wanted a repeat of that carnage. More important, how was he going to get everyone onboard with a plan to create a working system the organization desperately needed?

Richard required something more inclusive than cooperation to make this project work. He needed the stakeholders to be fully part of the actual solution. Consequently, he set out to get the stake- holders so engaged in the project that they would literally help him create it.

An additional challenge Richard faced (like he didn't have enough problems already) was that he wasn't the most diplomatic person. His natural style when people were being difficult was to verbally smack them upside the head and ask, "What the h-ll is wrong with you?!" That said, he was savvy enough to know that this would not achieve his goal.

Richard realized he needed to apply the lesson his mother had taught him about diplomacy in a far more sophisticated way than he ever had before—even more effectively than when he persuaded all the key stakeholders to abandon their legacy systems and go to one platform. So, he formulated a plan that would hopefully guide his organization into a co-creative process—one that would lead them out of the morass of conflict and frustration they were cur- rently stuck in.

He had had many experiences over his career that were helping to guide his thinking at this stage. One of the most salient was an exercise called the desert survival simulation, which he had used in a university course he taught for many years. In the simulation, people were given a theoretical situation where they were stranded in the desert, and they had to rank the items at hand that would help them survive. First they did the exercise individually, and then they were put in small groups to conduct the same process together. Almost every time, the groups scored higher in survivability than the indi- viduals. The point of the simulation was to demonstrate that small groups came to better conclusions than the average individual. Richard had used this approach in many small group settings over the years, but now it was time to ramp it up on a much grander scale.

There was a big conference coming up within the organization. Most of their franchisees and teams were going to be at this event.

But first, there was a meeting of the key stakeholders scheduled to take place. Richard knew this session could become another bloodbath if it wasn't handled properly and understood intuitively that this was a nexus point in his career. It could be a success, or it could be a disaster for the project and potentially the company itself. He also realized that before he could propose another plan, he needed to take responsibility for the failure of the project thus far and let them vent their frustration and anger. Only then would there be any chance of them coming together to co-create a solution.

As the conference drew closer, Richard learned that he needed the right focus, the right process, the right communication, and most important, the right execution for this project to succeed. But first, he had a rebellion to deal with.

The morning of the general session was the pre-conference meeting of the key leaders in the organization. There were about 35 of them, and they all came locked and loaded for the gathering. Richard stood at the front of the room and welcomed them all there. He felt a little like a lamb waiting to be sacrificed. But he also had a plan that could, just possibly, lead to a coming together of the minds (a focus) and then the creation of a process. Or it could lead to total chaos—he honestly wasn't sure. He was, however, certain of one thing: **This would either be the worst day of his professional career, or the best.**

CHAPTER 4

The Co-Creation Model
and the Four Knows

In recent years, some of the world's leading companies have implemented co-creation to increase productivity and creativity while decreasing employee turnover and costs. Yet that groundbreaking work, discussed by authors such as Venkat Ramaswamy and Francis Gouillart (*The Power of Co-Creation*), largely has not yet trickled down to smaller businesses. For every Nike, Lego, or Starbucks, there are thousands of smaller firms in need of a practical framework, backed by research, that leaders can implement.

We have known this for quite some time. In 1993, Michael Ray and Alan Rinzler co-edited the volume *The New Paradigm in Business: Emerging Strategies for Leadership and Organizational Change*. They acknowledged that while interest in co-creation was strong, "the world is not yet ready for an immediate move to that seemingly preferred mode of relationship." More recent work on co-creation has emerged out of necessity. Stefanie Jansen and Maarten Pieters confess that while on a project to co-create a new method for teaching Dutch children English, "the co-creation team had to overcome pretty much every barrier against co-creation." Their successful undertaking led them to write *The 7 Principles of Complete Co-Creation* in 2018 so others would have guidelines that were lacking during their own co-creative project.

Unlike 30 years ago, **the world is now ready for co-creation.** We have the technological capabilities and many examples of large enterprises that have embraced co-creation. It can be used for a specific project or as the basis of how an organization predominantly functions; either way, co-creation offers infinite possibilities.

Today, the world is facing pressing challenges that can only be solved by co-creation. We will not be able to overcome these challenges without it. And in response to the emerging urgency to understand the methodology of co-creation, we present the Co-Creation Model.

The Co-Creation Model

The Co-Creation Model is the cornerstone for what every business leader needs to know about implementing co-creation in their organization. You can see there are four basic components—what we call the "Four Knows." As Figure 4.1 below indicates, the area where each Know overlaps is where co-creation occurs.

Anyone trying to implement co-creation in their organization must understand each Know and its interdependency with the other three Knows. Co-creation will fail if all four are not in place and functioning effectively. Once you master the Four Knows, you will be well on your way to co-creating with your stakeholders.

But keep in mind that the Four Knows are not practiced in a vacuum. Co-creation is a skillful way of creating results that really matter to you and your stakeholders, so the entire process needs to be grounded in your core values. **How you treat people and why you get up in the morning is deeper than the Co-Creation Model, so make sure you identify the values you want to live by.**

We offer a cautionary tale from one of our survey respondents that illustrates how when just one of the Knows is missing, co-creation fails.

> I led a multidepartment high-profile supply chain logistics project to relocate our warehouse operations and install a conveyor system with automated picking. It was critical to relate to ALL levels

Figure 4.1 The Co-Creation Model

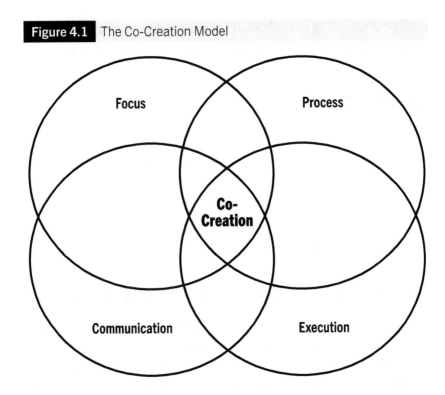

of staff and be likable. Handing out praise for the smallest things built our team up. Senior chiefs expected great results but lacked the ability to be inspiring to those working their normal jobs while juggling making this project come to a successful finish. We brought it in on time and under budget, and I wanted to PAUSE to have a huge celebration for the 100+ people who worked on it for 20 months. Instead, our senior vice president was hailed as brilliant, and business went on as usual. That lack of honoring the team resulted in deflated morale. Closure is very important to human beings who have bonded through trying times.

We suspect there were multiple issues at work here, but it's clear there was poor execution at the highest level in this example. The senior vice president's actions demonstrated that the project may have been successful according to traditional business metrics, but it fell far short in empowering employees and celebrating their accomplishment.

The Four Knows

No matter which of the five types of co-creation you use, you will need to have all four of the following in place to succeed:

1. Know the Right Focus
2. Know the Right Process
3. Know the Right Communication
4. Know the Right Execution

The Right Focus: Establish Mutually Desired Outcomes

Everyone involved in co-creation needs to be rowing in unison and in the same direction. This means everyone must be focused on a mutually desired outcome. Disaster strikes when people fail to work together, such as when one of our survey respondents shared how ineffective teamwork derailed their leaders' attempt to market an event: "We had not been able to communicate the WHY to them or get their views to make the event a part of the entire team."

How you treat people and why you get up in the morning is deeper than the Co-Creation Model, so make sure you identify the values you want to live by.

Focusing on the mutually desired outcome requires that all team members have a shared "why." Co-creation leaders can guide their teams through a series of questions that will help them work together efficiently, effectively, and creatively, even if they are composed of diverse stakeholders.

This process will help identify their right focus. The outcome cannot be vaguely defined—it must be clear. When it is, the co-creation stakeholders will have the necessary shared purpose and intention.

Once the mutually desired outcome is established, teams can accomplish the unthinkable. One survey respondent shared this sentiment: "If the right people, with the same goals, lifting, encouraging, and working together with the same commitment to achieve TOGETHER are in place, wonders can happen."

The Right Process: Implement a Framework

Identifying the right process for a co-creation project ensures stakeholders can work efficiently and effectively. It is not enough to have a team that is committed to a mutually desired outcome. Without an underlying process guiding the mission, frustrations will mount, and the project will become mired in problems.

The process of choosing a framework begins by selecting from the five types of co-creation we previously introduced (think tank/brainstorm, crowdsource, open source, mass customization, and user-generated content).

Once the co-creation leaders determine the right type, additional pragmatic considerations will provide the overarching framework and process. These include determining clear roles and responsibilities for team members, developing an accountability system, defining the situational context of the co-creation project, and mitigating unconscious bias.

Some survey respondents attested to the importance of having the right process: "All persons working on a project should be specifically responsible and accountable to some extent. All persons should be required to provide input." Others remarked on the importance of having "a good framework for growth in place" and the "need to be clear on the set tasks, with deadlines and people being responsible to either follow up with them or track the process." Defining the process can be at a granular level, such as one respondent who shared, "We used to have daily review meetings on the product development, so it helped us to have a close watch on the development process." Another recommended to "hold each member accountable for their piece of the process. Make sure the pieces fit moving into the next phase. Avoid backstepping."

The Right Communication: Ensure Open Communication

Open communication is crucial to successful co-creation. This must span employees, customers, vendors, and all of a company's other stakeholders. Without clear communication, co-creation will fail, even if everyone involved is passionate and fully engaged in the project. Many survey respondents underscored the importance of having the right communication:

"Communication is vital."

"I cannot say this enough: The better the communication you have with the people who work for you, the more successful your company will be."

"In companies where ideas are freely shared, a tremendous amount of growth happens. I have been at companies where the people in charge did not want to hear any ideas that weren't their own, so no growth happens there."

"[Co-creation] needs a lot of clear communication at every stage for the idea to develop properly."

"The larger the organization, the more there is a lack of communication about strategy and goals, which results in having no direction." [end]

One of our more memorable respondents wrote, "EVERYONE MUST BE SINGING OFF THE SAME SHEET OF MUSIC!!!!!" Indeed, a chorus full of enthusiastic singers each giving it their all will have a miserable time if everyone isn't performing the same song.

The Right Execution: Ensure Knowledgeable Leadership

Even with everything else in place—the right focus, the right process, and the right communication—all will be for naught if an organization lacks the right execution. Leaders of co-creation must lay the groundwork for successful empowerment and execution. With this final Know, leaders must have a clear plan and capably execute it while empowering stakeholders.

The entire process is at stake if the co-creative initiative falls short on execution. One survey respondent quipped, "Just a joke from my university days: When I die, I'd like the people I did group projects with to lower me into my grave, so they can let me down one last time." With the right execution, stakeholder morale soars; without it, disappointment abounds.

Stakeholders at the Center

Our Co-Creation Model inherently places stakeholder involvement in the center of each Know. In the broadest sense, stakeholders are people who have a relationship with the organization and an interest in the business succeeding. Your co-creative process will rely on active involvement from your stakeholders, although who they are varies widely depending on several factors.

For B2C organizations, stakeholders can include company owners, employees, direct consumers, the board of directors, advisory boards, vendors or suppliers, contractors or business resources (e.g., lawyers, accountants, web designers, IT support), referral partners, influencers, and anyone else who knows your business.

B2B organizations can have the same stakeholders as B2C companies, as well as employees, end users, and suppliers of their corporate clients or customers. For instance, stakeholders for a software firm would include companies that use their apps and other technology solutions.

For both B2B and B2C companies, stakeholders can include individuals and communities directly affected by the business' service offerings or products, even if they are not direct customers, employees, or vendors.

The size of a company also influences who its stakeholders are. In 2008 the federal government became a stakeholder in some of the country's largest banks (commonly referred to as "too big to fail") with the passage of the Emergency Economic Stabilization Act of 2008, commonly known as the bank bailout. Typically, the size of your business correlates to the number of your stakeholders, with small, family-run businesses generally having fewer stakeholders than large companies such as banks, airlines, oil and gas organizations, insurance firms, and auto manufacturers.

Bottom line: Involving varying stakeholders and identifying the roles the different types of stakeholders will play in co-creation is imperative. Some stakeholders might be crucial for effectively implementing new products, for instance, while others will be equally vital at the brainstorming stage.

THE STORY

We pick up with Richard's story at the conference, getting ready to face a few dozen of the key leaders in his organization. He had decided to put his key stakeholders in the center: engaging them, seeking their feedback, listening earnestly to their opinions, and processing their remarks thoughtfully. Now he would find out how well that would work for him.

Richard started the meeting right on time. He informed everyone in attendance that unlike past meetings, there was only one item on the agenda, the online platform, and that item would take up the entire three-and-a-half-hour meeting.

After he made that announcement, he stood nervously in front of the room and said:

"I want to apologize for what was released a few months ago. It was not what I promised it would be, and I take full responsibility for that. What I'd like for all of you to do is tell me everything you don't like about the platform. Everything. Don't leave anything out. I want to hear it all. As you share each issue with me, I'll write it on this flip chart. As I fill the pages up, I will have them taped up on the walls around you. We are going to go straight through the morning. I won't be stopping for breaks. If

*you need to get a cup of coffee or take a break, feel free to do
so, but I'm going to continue until you have shared everything
you want to about your frustration with this platform."*

This was Richard's **"Listen Till They Drop"** strategy. Let them
vent continuously for several hours. Do not interrupt them and, no
matter what, do not argue with them about any suggestions or complaints they share. In other words, shut up and keep calm. Do what
his friend Sam Horn called the ancient martial art of "tongue glue."
They needed to unleash their anger, and he needed to stay quiet
and listen—not exactly his natural strength.

Richard took each item as it came at him. One issue after
another. Each one he dutifully wrote onto the flip chart, number-
ing each of them as he went along. He completed page after page,
taping each one up on the wall until there were more than a hundred entries on multiple sheets posted. Then came the first lull. He
had expected this. The crowd needed to regroup and catch their
breath. He waited a few moments and said, "What else? What other
things are you unhappy with?" There was a short pause and then
they began to talk again, throwing complaint after complaint at
him. Most were totally legitimate, some were questionable, and a
few were petty and inconsequential. But it didn't matter, and he
definitely did not comment. He wrote each one down as though it
had equal weight.

After a couple hundred complaints, the group slowed down
again, and again Richard said, "What else? Surely this is not everything?" He was right. After a few moments one person spoke up,
and then another and another and another. The room was beginning to be wallpapered with flip charts listing every complaint people could think of. There were now close to 400 items on pages
filling most of the wall space in the room.

After two and a half hours, people were getting tired, but very
few wanted to leave because it was cathartic for them to get all this
frustration and anger out.

Finally, the room fell silent, and once again Richard asked, "What else? What else bothers you about the platform?" This time, they remained quiet. He had anticipated this, so he told his audience, "You can't call me a few weeks from now and say you didn't share *everything* that you were troubled about today. You cannot do that. I want to hear everything you can think of that you don't like about the system. Everything." He waited for 10 seconds, and the floodgates opened up again.

After three hours and more than 500 issues, a long silence finally fell over the room. The crowd was exhausted. They had nothing else to share. It was all on the table (or, in this case, on the walls). **His "Listen Till They Drop" strategy had allowed them to release their pent-up anger.** Maybe now everyone could focus on a solution.

And then Richard did something unexpected. He stood in front of the group and said, "Thank you. Thank you for being so honest and direct with your frustration about this platform. You were right to be upset, and I appreciate the issues that you listed for me here today." And then came the big question he'd been waiting for hours to ask: "Are you open to an idea that I have about this comprehensive list?"

The group was so tired and worn out by this point that they very softly agreed.

"Yes," someone said quietly. "Of course," said another, while nearly everyone nodded their assent.

Dawa

Books can be deceiving. To really understand a written idea, you have to trace it back to its origin. What insight, observation, or experience gave rise to the idea and the desire to share it? What observable natural order, system, or process lies at the root of the shared information?

When you can trace any text or concept back to the original insight or experience, you can start to work directly with the reality the book is trying to point to. But you don't want to mistake the book for the actual thing.

Texts can point to a realization, but they'll never replace it. When you see or learn a new model, such as the Co-Creation Model, don't stay on the surface; get into it and chomp at it, hack it back to its roots until you see right through it. That is when the magic starts, and you can make the insight your own. You end up where the author started, and you might even go much further. It's like a communion of the mind—you are no longer dependent on the book because you can read the world. Everything you could ever want to know is right there, right in front of you, always. That's like stepping into a library of practical wisdom and intelligence for which you do not need an access card. So use it. It is there for you.

Conclusion

The Four Knows that make up the Co-Creation Model make explicit what is implicit about the co-creative process. They break down what is required for a successful co-creative endeavor to succeed—and the visual model makes it clear that the Four Knows are interdependent.

The Co-Creation Model is a dynamic model. For co-creation to work, an organization must have each Know in place and be willing to adjust the focus, process, communication, and execution iteratively in response to stakeholder engagement. One survey respondent nicely summarized the opportunities and challenges of such a process:

I've seen both the good and bad sides of this issue and truly believe that group projects require strong vision and leadership to avoid it turning into an exercise in herding cats. With that strong vision, leadership, and a good framework for growth in place—having a diverse group of voices is invaluable. There are so many perspectives you could never possibly entertain as a single person or business entity. This diversity increases your creativity, amplifies your collective voice, and extends the reach of the final product, service, or idea. It just needs to be executed well!

Can this process feel messy? Yes. Can it feel stressful? Richard's case clearly demonstrates that it can. Is it worth it? Absolutely.

CHAPTER 5

The First Know: The Right Focus

This chapter provides key considerations to help you understand how to forge a mutually desired outcome among your team—and how to avoid the potholes created by silos and lack of shared vision.

When you initially bring a group of people together, apart from their physical features, there can be little that distinguishes them from any other group. Distinctions begin to emerge as they become organized around principles such as values, processes, and goals. This happens through communication and the development of shared understanding about what brought the group together in the first place and what they intend to do.

A powerful organizing principle that holds a key role in our model for co-creation (see Figure 5.1 below) is the mutually desired outcome: in other words, having the right focus. What outcome do people want to achieve from working together? Is there a desired goal or outcome shared by the members of a group that could distinguish this group from the next one? By sharing a unified focus, all co-creative team members can retain their individuality and continue to make their unique contributions while remaining focused on the goal at hand.

In the Co-Creation Model, a shared focus is key to achieving a successful co-creative process. It is so important that we have placed it as the first of the four key principles, or Four Knows, of our model. By

Figure 5.1 Co-Creation Model: The Right Focus

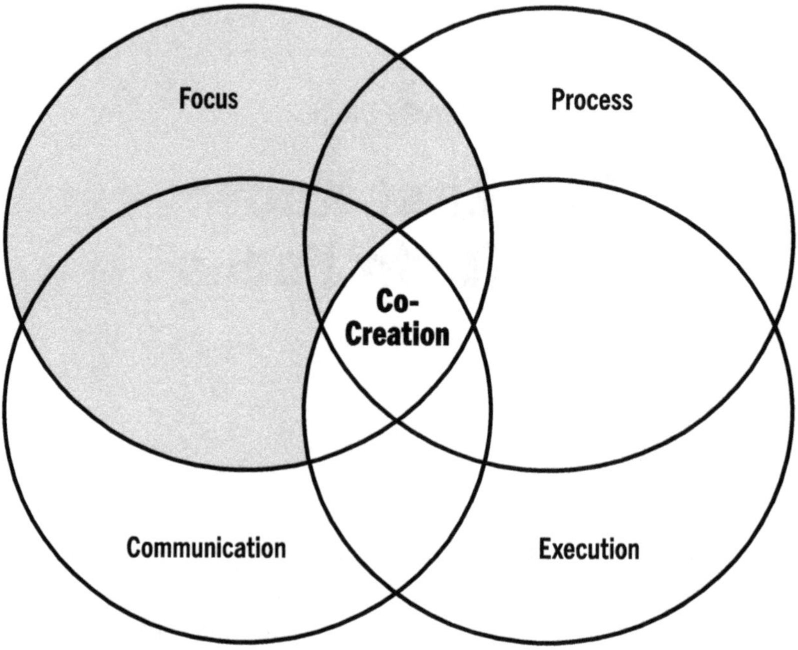

identifying organizing principles that might initially seem invisible or absent, we can provide support for shared meaning, intention, and motivation. These can serve as the foundation for individual commitments to a group effort. These commitments to achieving goals and outcomes that are desirable to everyone involved can create unique and unmatched results. We are inspired by British author Virginia Woolf, who wrote, "For masterpieces are not single and solitary births; they are the outcome of many years of thinking in common, of thinking by the body of the people, so that the experience of the mass is behind the single voice." This is what co-creation can generate with the power of shared focus.

Failed co-creative group processes, on the other hand, can be soul-crushingly destructive. Some recover only slowly from the best intentions, if they are devoid of a clear model, framework, and process. The experience can provoke strong emotions, as one of our survey participants conveyed:

I used to HATE group projects in school. People wouldn't pull their weight—you'd have to do your job and theirs to get a good grade. People would give you the "Yes, but" to your suggestions. Or worse, I would give a suggestion and it would be greeted with total silence, until someone else voiced the same thought and THEN it would be considered. Group projects even today give me PTSD.

These experiences are not uncommon but boil down to how well the process is structured, guided, and led.

Effective co-creation reflects good leadership at its best. Co-creative leadership demands clarity and capability upfront to make use of the right tools and sequential steps to get you and your team to the desired result. Deciding at the outset on a mutually desired outcome is critical.

Mutually Desired Outcome

Make sure you have a *mutually desired outcome* when you are co-creating with others. Therein lies both the opportunity and the challenge. A mutually desired outcome is more than just the result you will have to show for your effort. It includes the experiences you and your stakeholders will have along the way and will continue to have going forward once you reach your goal. That can seem counterintuitive in results-oriented cultures, which, due to their "ends justify the means" mindset, can neglect to pay attention to how they get results and the experience people have while achieving them. This can lead to unexpected collateral fallout.

A mutually desired outcome includes the *what, who, why, when, where,* and *how* of arriving at your destination. Often you can easily agree on what you want to achieve and still find that people have a million different ideas as to the meaning of that "what." The same goes for the *who, why, when* and *where.* And then there is the *how,* the actual *process* of achieving results, which if not carefully developed and managed can do your team or organization more harm than good.

Your outcome—and the journey you take to get to it—must be something that the people involved in the co-creative process can have a high investment in. They must be engaged.

The next stage of Richard's story illustrates how he worked to harness his stakeholders' ideas and energy to progress toward a co-creative solution. Throughout this process, he calmed their fears and assured them of his belief that they could work toward their solution—their mutually desired outcome—together.

After three hours of listening to their complaints (most of which were legitimate), Richard shared the plan that he had before he went into the meeting, but he knew better than to suggest it until everyone got their frustrations off their chest. He wanted the entire room to feel that their issues had been heard and treated with the respect they deserved.

"I have an idea," said Richard now. "I'd like us to create a project board, made up of some of the people in this room and a handful of others in the organization who are knowledgeable about the topic. This board will triage this extensive list of topics and pick the top 10 things to tackle first. Then the next 10, and the next 10, until we have completed every item on this list that the board feels needs to be addressed."

He added, "I will have no say in what items are given priority. If there is something that I want to focus on, I will allow the board to tackle it in the order that they want it addressed. I will give the board a budget, and they, along with franchisees, clients, and experts, will co-create a platform that we can all be proud of. This will be a true co-creative project. We will do it together."

The room was silent. Richard wasn't sure how the audience was receiving his proposal, but he was pleased that they hadn't had an immediate negative reaction, so he went on to the next step in his plan. He pulled out a big box filled with large buttons from under the table in front of him, took one out, and pinned it on his jacket. The button simply said: "EGBOK." His audience looked at him curiously.

He looked at them and shared his sincerest belief about this project: "Everything's Going to Be OK. EGBOK. We'll get through this. We will get through this because **all of us are better than one of us.** If we all work together to address these issues, we will create, together, a platform that will be a game changer for the company. Everything's Going to Be OK. We can do this. Now, who wants to volunteer for the project board, and who else do you recommend who is not here today?"

He watched with immense relief as people began volunteering to serve on the board and others made great suggestions about who else should be on it. By the end of the meeting (some three and a half hours after it began), they had created a list of issues to investigate and put a plan in place. More important, there was a general sense of relief and accomplishment in the room. There was a sincere belief that the group, as a whole, could find a solution to the many problems the organization faced with this new venture. **The tidal wave of anger had transitioned to the stillness of confidence.** This was a productive meeting.

Finally, Richard asked everyone, "Who would like some buttons? Take a handful and pass them out to other people in the organization who are concerned. Let them know: You've been heard, and we have a plan. **Everything's Going to Be OK. EGBOK.**" He once again thanked everyone and asked those who had volunteered for the board to stick around so they could talk in a few minutes. He watched as the meeting participants filed out of the room one by one clutching handfuls of the buttons. There were people standing outside waiting for the meeting to end so they could find out what had happened. The participants gave person after person the buttons and told them, "We have a plan. *Everything's Going to Be OK. EGBOK.*" He noticed with a little smile that some people were responding: "Say what? What happened in there? How is everything going to be OK? Didn't you tell him how upset we are? What's the plan?" He then watched with pride how the participants explained what went on at the meeting and why they now believed that every-thing was going to be fine.

Richard had trained for years in martial arts and learned of a movement called "*Tenkan,*" which is taught in karate, aikido, and judo (among other styles). *Tenkan* means to convert or divert someone by taking their momentum and pivoting with them 180 degrees. His approach that day was very similar. He had embraced their anger and pivoted with them to find a solution.

Now he was relieved. What could have been the worst day of his career might just prove to be the best one. The plan was in place. Soon the real work of co-creation would begin. Richard realized that the process would be messy, difficult, and frustrating—but he also knew it could work.

After the meeting, Richard walked to the auditorium, where the general session was scheduled to begin in an hour, and began to execute the next parts of his plan. The first stage was to meet and greet the franchisees and their staff as they mingled outside the room. A conflict resolution consultant had advised him to be con-scious of his facial expressions and body language. He was told to walk slowly around the convention floor and smile like Gandhi. So he strolled around the event nodding at everyone with a quiet, confident smile. He shook hands with people as he passed and qui-etly reassured the people he spoke to that everything would be OK. Richard knew that **leading a co-creative process had to begin by presenting quiet confidence while showing a belief in the ability of all those around him to contribute to the end result.** That way, he could draw everyone into a place where they could focus on solu-tions, not problems. That is a key piece of the co-creative process.

The What, Who, Why, When, Where, and How of Achieving a Mutually Desired Outcome

When you take time at the outset to properly define a mutually desired outcome, it will go a long way toward uniting people and creating a process that they will feel excited about—and can commit to. To illustrate this, let's take two individuals, Sam and Fred. Both are hungry. Their mutually desired outcome is that they both want to make dinner and eat. But Sam wants barbecue, and Fred wants sushi. If you fail to align their outcome with enough specifics, it can leave the process trapped in misunderstandings, frustration, disappointment, and grievances.

If you aspire to successful co-creation, allot adequate time to identifying the mutually desired outcome and making sure everyone understands it. If you add enough specifics to clear up all lingering misconceptions and misunderstandings, the process of co-creation will go much more smoothly.

The outcome—the *what*—is only part of the equation when it comes to effective co-creation. It also matters *who, why, when, where,* and *how* you and your co-creators want to achieve the mutually desired outcome. In other words, the people involved and their daily experience of the process matter, too.

Leading a co-creative process had to begin by presenting quiet confidence while showing a belief in the ability of all those around him to contribute to the end result.

If, for example, the desired outcome is clear but not the stakeholders involved (the *who*), the result might fall short of meeting the wants and needs of the people it should serve.

Similarly, if the outcome is clear but not the reason for doing it (the *why*), people might employ methods for achieving the outcome that are out of alignment with your organization's integrity and values.

If the outcome is clear but not the timing (the *when*), people might get frustrated by the pressure behind the project, or by the lack of expediency invested or progress made.

If the outcome is clear but not the location for the project (the *where*), people might wrangle for home turf advantage or push the project into an area that's disadvantageous to its completion.

And if the outcome is clear but not the process (the *how*), that can easily derail and sabotage an otherwise meaningful and promising co-creation. That's why it's important to clearly define the process through which a successful outcome can be achieved. This includes understanding who is responsible for what, when activities should take place, and how decisions will be made. It also involves agreeing on the tools that will be used throughout the co-creation process and creating a timeline that outlines key milestones and deadlines.

As the proverb states, "If you fail to prepare, you are preparing to fail." Take the time you need and keep working at the mutually desired outcome—on the level of what, who, why, when, where, and how—until you and your team are ready to sign off on the plan.

Especially for visionary leaders, it is important to pay attention to how many people share the vision they are pursuing through co-creation. Failing to get sufficient buy-in has brought many co-creative processes to a halt before significant progress could be made. This is where going the extra mile in planning can mean the difference between success and failure. Later in the co-creative process, reminding people of the shared vision and mutually desired outcome allows you to overcome difficulties and hold egos in check, which were both common complaints from our survey participants. One person succinctly stated, "Lack of communication, misaligned intentions, and egos can disrupt positive flow." Another detailed a common, problematic occurrence at work, which could have been remedied with a stronger co-creative approach:

> I used to work where teams were divided between Business and IT. Business teams would come up with product requirements on the system that could be offered to customers, and IT would develop the product with its features in the system. More often than not, the Business team would assume that their ideas would be disruptive and would revolutionize the industry. Only after the implementation, two years later, would it be acknowledged that technology had changed and the product was totally outdated and had no takers.

If you are choosing *Think tank/brainstorm* as your method of co-creation, look at how your defined outcome meets the wants and needs of those involved in the brainstorming process and how the process itself is set up to provide a high degree of satisfaction to the participants.

If *Crowdsource* is your choice, look at how transparently you are communicating, and give people an opportunity to be involved not just during the early stages but along the entire process of going from initial idea to finished product, service, or market entry.

If you decide to use *Open source* to deepen your understanding and capacity for co-creation, what could a long-term, mutually desirable outcome look like to all those who are making their unique thinking and processes available to you? What systems of governance and decision making might be needed to protect their generosity and vulnerability?

During a *Mass customization* co-creative process, it might be key to look at how shared values such as freedom of speech or freedom of expression might underlie a desire for individualization and unique expression as *mutually desired goals.*

User-generated content is perhaps the most confounding of the co-creative approaches, as it partially meets our desire for community while at the same time risks exposing us to the feelings of inadequacy, disenfranchisement, and disconnect associated with the use of social media platforms. Consider what balance might need to be struck to maximize its benefits and minimize the downsides of social media.

Why Intention Matters

The first thing you "scan" for when you walk into a room or a meeting is the atmosphere in that room. Your personal radar reads very quickly the energy of the environment and picks up on the general intentions of those around you.

Am I safe here? Am I among friends? Can I let my guard down and be myself? Can I speak freely? Or do I need to be vigilant? Do I need to protect myself? Do I need to look out for hidden meanings or traps? These are the questions your subconscious mind will try to answer in just the first few milliseconds of being in a new environment with other people.

Dawa

One of my teachers used to tell the following story, which illustrates clearly how intention can influence outcomes. He would say, "Think of two neighbors who live side by side on adjacent properties. Both love to see things grow in their garden and wish to plant a tree—a fruit tree, to be exact. One neighbor plants her fruit tree in her front yard and nurtures and waters it carefully. She tends to it with great skill and patience because she knows that the tree will grow and flower and that one day she will get to enjoy the many sweet and tasty fruits it will produce.

The other neighbor plants her tree in front of her property as well, but she plants it just outside her fence. She nurtures and waters it in the same way. She, too, cares for it with great skill and patience because she knows that the tree will grow and flower and that one day everyone who passes by her property will get to enjoy the many sweet and tasty fruits that it will produce.

Both neighbors do exactly the same work, care for their trees in exactly the same way, and put in exactly as many hours, but the results are completely different—and so can be their ultimate level of gratification. That is the power of intention."

This story and my own practice of leadership have taught me to be especially mindful of intention, because it is a major game changer in the way we create results in our lives and the level of reach and impact our actions can unfold.

Therefore, **developing a shared intention and meaning is vital to establishing an atmosphere of trust,** in which each person can tell that they are being allowed sufficient room to expand, be authentic, and have input and ownership of the co-creative process and its results.

You have to take shared meaning and intention into account from the beginning. What does it mean for each person in the process to be involved in the project? Why did they come onboard? What experiences and outcomes do they hope to achieve? What are they hoping to avoid?

When starting up a new company, for example, one co-creator/ founder might be approaching the project with the intention of selling the company in three to five years, while another co-creator might be hoping that the company will be their legacy, something that will be associated with their family name for generations to come. Selling a company quickly or building a legacy project are very different motivations, even though both co-creators want their company to succeed.

These different reasons, intentions, and motivations are evident in the daily decision-making process, which can get slowed down or obstructed. The process can even fail before it ever gets a chance to really take off.

That is why it is important for co-creators to not only discuss their mutually desired outcome but also choose a co-creative process together, decide who needs to be involved when and where, and assess their intentions behind the co-creation. Ask yourself: What are everyone's drivers and motives, and where is there alignment that can make the process enjoyable and successful for all involved?

Intention is a known variable that you should take into account when you are co-creating. In *The Intention Experiment* (2007), science-writer Lynne McTaggart demonstrated how powerful intention can be in all areas of our lives and how it can demonstratively influence animate and inanimate objects and circumstances in our surroundings, using research from such leading institutions as MIT, Princeton University, and Stanford University. Since publication, she has continued to work with teams of scientists to test theories of mass intention, an intention directed at an outcome held and shared by a large group of people. According to McTaggart, 35 of 39 experiments have "evidenced positive, measurable, mostly significant change." When it comes to co-creation in business, clarity of intent is crucial because it helps bring all stakeholders together.

And despite frequent headwinds, shared intent can help make co-creation a meaningful and empowering experience. One survey respondent, a property lawyer, reported:

I experienced co-creation working with my all-women team on the new structure of activities, responsibilities, goals, and the future of our department. We are all of different ages, but all of us share the passion for intellectual property and therefore without egos decided how the different work/areas will be divided. Everyone is always telling me that it is hard to work with just women, but for me it has been fantastic since we are clear about our final goal: working on IP and learning from each other!

The clearer and more open about our intention we are as we begin the co-creative process, the better our chances are for a successful experience. How have you seen intention impact the results in your own life? How have you responded to the perceived intentions of others?

Intention and Survey Results

Our survey results reveal distinctions when it comes to how groups of different sizes manage the co-creative process and how exposed they are to the risk of having their project hijacked by people with different intentions. We found that small groups under 10 and large groups over 100 were especially prone to this issue (see Figure 5.2 below).

Small groups of less than 10 and large groups of more than 100 people are more likely to have the project hijacked by an individual with a

Figure 5.2 Number of People in the Organization by Top 7 Drawbacks

Number of people in organization	10 or fewer	11 – 100	Over 100
Personality conflicts	58.72%	57.17%	57.80%
Dealing with egos	57.18%	58.50%	55.80%
Poor communication	41.72%	38.83%	38.80%
People who don't pull their weight	40.87%	37.09%	38.0%
Lack of agreement on who makes the final decision	36.55%	38.42%	36.40%
Individuals hijacking the project direction	37.06%	32.17%	37.20%
Non-aligned vision of the project	33.58%	33.81%	32.0%

different intention than a midsize group (11 to 100 people). This might be due to the ability to delegate responsibility and authority more easily in groups of that size. Or people in those groups might find it easier to feel that they are members of a collective, with a mandate to act accordingly.

Get Clear on Your Common Pain Points

Everyone struggles; it is part of being human. When there is a problem to be solved, you can be sure that somewhere it is causing someone pain. Good business is built on solving problems and alleviating that pain.

What pain points are driving your team? What struggles and challenges are making the co-creation—and its success—not just a privilege, but a necessity? Every business has different departments handling separate tasks: marketing and sales, operations, finance, HR, IT, etc. **Even in the best scenario, in a business where everyone is focused on doing their job well, problems occur. Processes get jammed and systems get compromised.** When that happens, sooner or later everyone suffers, from senior management all the way to the client and customer. And it becomes increasingly difficult for everyone to get their job done.

Google CEO Sundar Pichai knows a thing or two about this, which is why he has made it a point to frequently survey employees to help the company boost its productivity. Google called the process, launched in 2022, a "Simplicity Sprint," and it included surveying all 176,000 employees. The executives then sifted through the responses and contacted those employees who offered ideas that Google could shape into valuable policy.

Common pain points arise where people are working together to solve problems. Because of the complex, interdependent nature of most problems, they generally cannot be solved by telling employees to get their act together and suck it up. A more collaborative and co-creative approach is required to lift the entire team or company ecosystem to a new level of functioning and higher performance, or to remove the problem at its root.

If you can bond over your common pain points, you will be able to co-create together to overcome your challenges and the pains they are causing. **Co-creation does not mean you are neglecting the individual.** Everyone has a right to their own opinion, and, in successful co-creation, everyone's opinion matters. You want people to feel empowered and confident to speak up and to speak their mind.

Even in the best scenario, in a business where everyone is focused on doing their job well, problems occur. Processes get jammed and systems get compromised.

You need to hear not only what your greatest fans have to say, but also what your greatest skeptics and critics have to offer. This is not because you want to let those objections obstruct the process or limit your possibilities, but because there are weaknesses, challenges, and drawbacks to every situation. Co-creation incorporates all that into the process of generating an innovative and valuable solution.

H2 Clipper is an innovative and disruptive hydrogen transport and distribution company in Santa Barbara, California, that builds new technologies to help mitigate the effects of climate change. Founder and CEO Rinaldo Brutoco, who we interviewed for this book, is no stranger to the 3rd Paradigm of Co-Creation and how it drastically differs from the 1st and 2nd Paradigms of competition and cooperation:

When I entered the business world, having just graduated from law school, I was steeped in what's called the tradition of competition. We venerated competition, not just in the West, frankly, but even in the East. We didn't understand that there were alternatives because we saw the benefits of competition. In the United States, in part due to professional sports, we think of competition as the preferred methodology for achieving success and rewards, financial and otherwise.

It became apparent to me fairly quickly that that was OK, but it didn't go far enough. Most often, competition deteriorates into zero-sum thinking: I win, you lose. That kind of competition tends to block creativity. So I said, "OK, what's better than competition if it's not perfect in all cases?" And the answer that came up was cooperation. That was a very powerful learning—that competition represents forces clashing and cooperation brings forces into parallel.

For co-creation, we went even further. Co-creation is forces being in fusion. This is when two plus two can become more than the sum of its parts; two plus two can become five. The difference between being in parallel and fusion implies significant new outcomes. Co-creation creates significant new outcomes that you don't get with parallel forces or with competition. When I understood that, I started looking with different eyes at what we do in business. Cooperation can often lead to two plus two equals four and a half. But to get to five, you've got to co-create, you've got to have co-creators.

My mother was a simple woman, but she had a lot of wisdom. And one of [her sayings] was that "Many hands make light work." It's easier when you have more people engaged. If you can find many hands to make light of the work, and if you can enjoy the co-creative spirit of those hands, joined in common enterprise with common objective, then it becomes a wonderful way to live, not just to work.

Common Pain Points and Survey Results

Different generations engage in co-creation to address different pain points, and for different reasons, and they experience wide-ranging benefits from the co-creative process. Our survey results suggest that as people age, the sense of empowerment and shared ownership becomes more important to them (see Figure 5.3 below). This might be because as we grow older, we value different aspects of working with others than we do when we are young. If so, a disparate yet clearer picture of the interpersonal value of working with others could begin to emerge.

Younger generations appear to value the increased creativity and the shared resources more, which our survey suggests begins to diminish somewhat with older generations. What can this tell us about the emergence of the 3rd Paradigm and its surge in popularity? We believe the

Figure 5.3 Age by Top 7 Benefits

Age	29 or under	30 – 39	40 – 49	50 – 59	60 or over
Diversity of ideas	73.46%	67.83%	67.58%	68.88%	72.05%
Learning from each other	67.77%	63.59%	63.72%	59.58%	60.48%
Stronger relationships	45.50%	49.0%	46.74%	51.90%	52.99%
Seeing areas of the business that you don't see	47.87%	50.75%	46.74%	49.56%	50.19%
More empowered team/shared feeling of ownership	37.91%	42.14%	44.60%	51.58%	51.21%
Increased quality of creativity	54.03%	47.13%	46.83%	44.62%	48.16%
Shared resources	56.87%	46.38%	46.31%	43.90%	44.85%

future of co-creation is significant and promising as it continues to gain traction in various industries. Co-creation allows for collaboration and innovation, leading to the development of more tailored and effective products and services. With the rise of technology and globalization, co-creation is almost certainly going to become even more prevalent and essential in creating sustainable solutions for the future.

Interestingly, baby boomers and Gen Xers are more likely to feel more of a sense of empowerment or ownership in the co-creative process than Millennials or Gen Zers. On the other hand, Gen Z and younger Millennials are more likely to see an increased quality of creativity and more shared resources than Gen Xers and baby boomers (we will discuss the latter in more detail in Chapter 8). While co-creation is appreciated by people of all ages, it is not always under the same circumstances or for the same reasons.

Build a Common Vision

To bring the mutually desired outcome to life for everyone, you must be able to describe it in vivid, emotive terms. How will it look to achieve the outcome? What impact will it have on the business and its stakeholders? What impact will it have on your own life? How do you anticipate you will feel when your team reaches its goal?

The late Tony Hsieh, retired visionary CEO of online shoe retailer Zappos.com, used to say, "Chase the vision, not the money; the money will end up following you." Tony had his own struggles, but he used his company, which exemplified and united around strong customer service, as an example of this principle.

Storytelling can aid in building your vision. Since the human mind thinks in both pictures and words, the more vividly you can describe what you are co-creating, the easier it will be for people to grasp. Abstract concepts hold little food for the imagination, but descriptions offer plenty of opportunity to see ourselves as part of something larger.

A strong vision grounded in commonalities shared by all stakeholders is a no-brainer for people to join. On this topic, one survey respondent shared the following story:

> I was coproducing a workshop with a very talented and well-known woman, and I was so excited!...[But] we had inconsistent philosophies and wanted very different things from it, thus producing very different visions of the outcome. Visioning has to be a core component of collaborative work—you have to be headed in the same direction, otherwise you don't have a clear message to deliver.

Clearly a strong vision maximizes the available intention, interest, and commitment toward achievement by drawing on the inherent and natural drives and motives of the people involved.

Contribute in Service to Others

In business, you will often come up against self-interest, whether it's your own or other people's. Some economists believe that letting self-interest operate freely is what open, self-regulating markets are all about. This is only partially true, however, because every company is an ecosystem of funders, producers, vendors, marketers, consumers, and many other people who are required to make a business successful. The interdependence among all stakeholders of a business means you must make the effort to think outside your limited perspective of self.

When you are interested in greater service to your stakeholders and society as a whole, you will be well-positioned to grow beyond the 1st and 2nd Paradigms and develop a mature understanding of the 3rd Paradigm.

Legacy businesses that still operate according to the 1st and 2nd Paradigms may struggle to compete with disruptive modern companies that have harnessed the power of co-creation.

The 1st and 2nd Paradigms are limited by both their intention and their approach to success because fewer people are involved in creating value in comparison with the 3rd Paradigm. **Legacy businesses that still operate according to the 1st and 2nd Paradigms may struggle to compete with disruptive modern companies that have harnessed the power of co-creation.**

Competition works on a win/lose model, in which one person's success almost always means a defeat for someone else. Cooperation is based on telling groups of people what to do and how to do it. But co-creation is built on accessing an intention and vision that are much vaster and deeper in scope and power. While it is skillfully used to optimize products and services your customers want and need, it is also a powerful tool for harnessing the energy of people who are genuinely interested in serving others, in a more interconnected, unselfish, and responsible way. This transformative power of co-creation is still in its infancy but could represent hope for the future in an often divided and conflicted world.

Take a parent, for example. Once a parent has accepted responsibility for their child, they learn to not only provide food and shelter, but also supply clothing, health care, education, and recreational activities, all while taking on hardships, trying to take care of themselves, and working to earn money so that the lights stay on in the home.

Their love, care, and sense of personal responsibility for the child's welfare drive parents to **go beyond what is comfortable and into *what*** *is necessary.* And that is often to put your self-interest aside and start thinking about the bigger picture.

Organizations and leaders that have embraced the 3rd Paradigm can make that shift. They put their personal preferences aside and look at what the situation really requires to develop into the next phase of successful evolution. Their intention focuses on the success of the project and the co-creative process rather than on self-interest or personal disconnect. Everyone involved concentrates on the greater good by accessing the synergy that exists between the different stakeholders, which is only possible when people work together in a true spirit of co-creation. **Co-creation is about contributing in ways no one could ever imagine alone.**

To realize that goal, you must keep the intention of being of service foremost in your mind. When this happens, no one is trying to dominate or hijack the process because they recognize they are all part of a larger ecosystem of interdependent stakeholders. And why would they bother? Market trends suggest everything will ultimately work in their favor.

According to Brutoco, effective co-creation requires several attitude shifts:

> Check your ego at the door. Be careful not to be so stuck that you think you know everything, and nobody else knows even close to what you know. Because then there's nothing for them to add. To become a great businessperson, you've got to let your ego go. You might think the guy sitting across the desk is just a peasant while you're the pope, but that person has something important to teach you, and it is your job to figure out what that is. Almost everybody has something to add.
>
> You've got to be willing to model what you're asking for from others, and you've got to be willing to model what you stand for. Be curious. The vast majority of us are social animals; we want to be in relationships. Co-creation in business is the highest form of relationship and therefore provides the greatest amount of satisfaction. When you know what you want to be able to look back on later in life, it is not just a series of material triumphs.

You want to feel good about the difference you've made and about your spiritual journey—and hope it has prepared you for whatever comes next in the best possible way. If you keep that in mind, co-creation doesn't just become a question—it becomes an inevitability.

Brutoco highlights something that often goes unsaid: Co-creation doesn't just lead to a positive business result but also to a personal benefit. Even though other approaches can sometimes get results faster, participants consider the 3rd Paradigm a valuable pursuit that can have a permanent effect on them personally. In other words, **personal growth is a byproduct of the co-creative process.**

The qualities that emerge in individuals and organizations as they progress from the 1st to the 2nd and finally through the 3rd Paradigm reflect an important human development that every generation hopes to pass on to the next: a better life, and a better world. Can we find signs that point to us achieving those ambitious goals? In Chapter 8, we discuss data from our survey regarding differences in generational appreciation for co-creation. One insight that our data revealed is that co-creation is an emerging trend among younger generations, just as it is an emerging trend among modern businesses. Baby boomers resisted co-creation more than any other age group, and the youngest respondents (Gen Zers) resisted it the least, indicating that a shift is afoot in the way businesses and the people in them are thinking about work.

Accept Stewardship for the Whole

In co-creation, no one is a spectator. Everyone is a creator, and thereby responsible for the final result. That means that you are just as responsible for the intention, the culture, and the execution as the next person or leader on the team. You need to take responsibility for the whole and not just for your individual piece, however large or small it may be. When you begin to care for the health and well-being of the whole, you become a living part of the project—or the organization.

Co-creation represents a paradigm shift in more than just the means of productivity. It is an attempt to address more effectively the most complex problems of our time—problems like global pandemics, climate change, mass migration, access to food and water, the proliferation of the military-industrial complex, trade, currency, and class wars, to name a few. These problems are complex, and in an increasingly interconnected and interdependent world, co-creation could represent the next evolutionary threshold of our problem-solving capability.

Let's take a look at how the world responded to COVID-19. Within weeks of the first outbreak in early 2020, scientists started sharing research data and companies around the world started co-creating solutions to the shortage of face masks and other medical supplies. Reviewing the global supply chain for the most in-demand items, businesspeople around the world began retooling factories and innovating solutions like 3D-printed face shields and mass-producing gloves and portable disinfectants. It gave us a glimpse of what might be possible if co-creation were to be applied among nations and governments in response to climate change or food and water shortages.

Co-creation represents a paradigm shift in more than just the means of productivity. It is an attempt to address more effectively the most complex problems of our time.

Anthropologists have theorized that what has enabled humans to dominate over other species in the world is the ability to collaborate in tribes and operate at scale. If humanity hopes to survive its own exponential expansion, it must rely on its ability to co-create.

Key to this is for each of us as individuals to accept our stewardship of—and responsibility for—the whole. We can learn to look at humanity and the world as one integrated system that can overcome its challenges through collective evolution and co-creation, rather than viewing it as fragmented, individual battles for survival. The first two paradigms—competition and cooperation—simply do not provide us with enough synergy and momentum to address the enormous problems (and opportunities) we currently face. **The 3rd Paradigm of**

Co-Creation not only can help businesses more effectively address the challenges of a complex marketplace, but it can also become a vital tool for humanity's problem-solving abilities on a global scale.

Commit to Measurable Outcomes

Successful co-creation requires commitment and the ability to clearly measure progress and completion of the project or task. How do you know when you have finished what you set out to do? What are the markers of progress that signal your outcome was achieved? You could not commit to completing a marathon if you did not know the race was 26.2 miles long. You would not be able to improve your performance if you did not track your running time. Commitment is not the endpoint but the starting point. It creates accountability, which forces people to confront their usual habits, despite their discomfort, and keeps them on track toward meeting their goal.

Outcomes must be measurable to have accountability. **You cannot improve what you cannot measure.** Decide where your finish line should be so you know how to measure your progress. When you think about the outcomes you want to create, also think about whether you will be able to measure them, and how you will be able to know that you have successfully met your goal.

Determine Your Metrics

What does accountability look like? Someone has to lead the process—not the result, but the process. Decide what you are going to measure, and then decide who is responsible for meeting each milestone and the result you are hoping to achieve together. **Accountability is created when you know *who will do what by when*.** The person taking on the task should be the one clearly stating that they will do X (task) by Y (date/time), or you will have no accountability.

Assigning roles and responsibilities to someone does not yet constitute accountability, as the person charged with a task may not agree.

Only when they have given verbal confirmation or written buy-in and commitment to the task and the deadline do you have a mechanism for accountability.

Let's look again at our friends Sam and Fred from the beginning of this chapter. (Remember that both are hungry, but Sam wanted barbecue and Fred wanted sushi.) Sam could claim that Fred said he would make barbecue for dinner, but if Fred never agreed to do so, there is no way to hold him accountable to his word. Alternatively, if Sam did not tell Fred he is going to make sushi for the two of them, there is no mechanism in place to hold him accountable to his word to do so either. **You can only hold someone accountable for what *they* said they would do and haven't yet done, not for something you thought they should do but that they never agreed to.**

You can only hold someone accountable for what *they* said they would do and haven't yet done, not for something you thought they should do but that they never agreed to.

Decide what you want accountability to look like for your project. Is everyone accountable to the same degree? Should one person be accountable for making sure milestones are met and report back on them to the rest of the group?

Determine Your Flexible Boundaries

Many things that are rigid are weak. And things that have no boundaries or structure are untenable and will eventually fall into chaos. The sweet spot of effectiveness and efficiency lies somewhere in the middle. As a result, healthy, strong, yet flexible boundaries are essential to succeed in business. You will need to be aware of the times when you must adapt, pivot, and relax your boundaries to draw new, more efficient ones. Identify the flexible boundaries that you and your project need to succeed. How can you establish, maintain, and communicate them to everyone involved?

One way to establish flexible boundaries but keep them under control is by using time constraints. Limit the amount of time that people can contribute in each phase of the co-creative process. This creates a sense of urgency that compels people to act sooner and get their part of the project done more efficiently.

Another way to control your boundaries is by using space. Limit the physical location where people can contribute to the co-creation. This can also limit the amount of data that will be collected, reviewed, and integrated into the project.

You can also set boundaries by limiting the size and scope of the project, and, by doing so, establishing fixed parameters for how people can and will go about the mutually desired outcome you are trying to create.

By using time, space, size, and scope, you can set flexible boundaries and keep your project manageable, giving it both the structure and adaptability it needs to succeed.

Conclusion

Take time early in the co-creative process to get clear about what has brought you together with others and what you want to achieve; also clarify when, where, why, and how you want to achieve it. Co-creation can be messy, but it is not without focus, commitment, and intent. If you do the work, you can set the stage for a strong and successful co-creative journey by addressing the first part of the Co-Creation Model: the right focus. This means getting and staying focused on a mutually desired outcome.

CHAPTER 6

The Second Know: The Right Process

As the previous chapter laid out, it is important to understand where you are going—your focus—before you can determine how you will get there. This chapter is about the latter, identifying your process for engaging in co-creation in order to make steady progress toward achieving your mutually desired outcome. See Figure 6.1 below.

Process and Structure

As one of the biggest consumer goods companies in the world, Unilever owns more than 400 well-known brands, including Dove, Lipton, Ben & Jerry's and many others.

Unilever has operations in 190 nations and its products are used daily by over 2.5 billion people, giving it access to a sizable customer base that can be used to generate ideas and find answers to product development problems.

Unilever presents specific challenges to the public through its Open Innovation platform and actively seeks product solutions from its customer base, consulting with startups, researchers, designers, and customers for ideas and suggestions.

Figure 6.1 Co-Creation Model: The Right Process

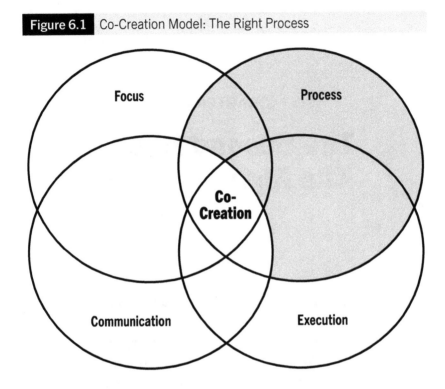

These include things like cutting-edge oil oxidation technology, freezing and cooling systems, and intelligent product packaging, among other things, and a commercial contract for the suggested solution, as well as professional recognition, may be made available to the submitter if the idea is accepted. Over 60 percent of Unilever's research projects now involve external collaboration, a result of this strategy's contribution.

When undertaking co-creation, with its clear potential upsides, it is easy to get lost in the weeds or lose sight of your objective. This is often due to a lack of clear structure and effective process. You may get overwhelmed and try to take shortcuts, or try to gather too much information without a clear way of synthesizing it into actionable steps and forward momentum.

Many brilliant people fail to consider the value of boundaries and limitations in co-creation or seem unwilling to impose them for the sake of greater clarity and precision. It's a common but avoidable mistake.

The human brain has a limited aptitude for absorbing, retaining, and processing information, and it is still considered the smartest and fastest processing system we know. Take human *working memory capacity*, for example, the brain's ability to retain, access, and process input. In trying to retain too much information in our working memory alone, we often get lost, overwhelmed, and forgetful. We drop the ball. This causes bottlenecks, dysfunction, or slowdowns.

Similar things can happen when you embark on co-creation without a clear process or model to follow. You can get bogged down, and your progress gets slowed.

In our survey, 30 percent of participants named *too many ideas* as a major drawback to co-creation. To avoid the confusion that can stem from too many cooks in the kitchen, we recommend that you choose a clear process you can easily follow early on, and then do your best to stick to it. This allows you and your team to employ co-creation methods following clear, proven steps and progressive stages. You can rinse and repeat the process as many times as you want, while staying on target and on track.

Think of a river. It constantly re-creates itself, but it does so within the controlled environment of the riverbed. Lacking that riverbed, it would not qualify as a river any longer—you would likely call it just a "floodplain." The riverbed provides structure, restrictions, and limitations, supporting the dynamic, creative flow and force of the water with enough directionality and focus to keep driving it forward. This forward momentum generates power that can be harnessed for value creation, from watering fields and clearing biomass to shipping goods and generating hydropower.

That is part of what makes rivers so valuable to us. More than 50 percent of the world's population lives closer than 1.8 miles to a surface freshwater body, and only 10 percent of the population lives farther than 6.2 miles away. Water is not just life; it is power.

Both the supporting structure (the riverbed) and the directional process (the moving water mass) are needed to give the river its value. This is also how co-creation can and should function in business. Think of

Dr. Martin Luther King Jr.'s words, "Whatever affects one directly, affects all indirectly. For some strange reason I can never be what I ought to be until you are what you ought to be. . . . This is the interrelated structure of reality." We have to take the interconnected parts of the big picture into account to get the momentum we want.

During co-creation, rely on a strong support structure and a sequential process to help you move through and generate the value and innovative renewal that can come from this 3rd Paradigm approach.

Determine Your Co-Creation Structure

In Chapter 2, we discussed five different popular types of co-creation: think tank/brainstorm, crowdsource, open source, mass customization, and user-generated content.

1. *Think tank/brainstorm:* A group or company brings together a consortium of people, experts, suppliers, and/or partners to develop a new solution, product, or service.

2. *Crowdsource:* A large group of people (often volunteers) co-create (often for free) a product or service. This usually happens via the internet, using web-based co-creative tools.

3. *Open source:* A group or company invites a large group of internal and external experts to tackle its innovation challenge or contribute to its data pool.

4. *Mass customization:* A group or company mass-produces products that have been individually tailored to the customer's personal wishes.

5. *User-generated content:* A group or company uses knowledge and content that has been made publicly available by people (e.g., posted online).

Which one you choose is up to you. Time, place, size, scope, and personnel constraints, as well as desired outcomes, favor some approaches over others. Your overarching process for co-creation will be influenced by which framework, or type of co-creation, you decide to use.

All these approaches represent a shift in the relationship and power dynamics between businesses and their customers and consumers. Rather than customers and other stakeholders remaining outside the value creation process as mere recipients and consumers, the joint creation of value by the company and the customer, which invites the customer in and empowers them to co-construct the product or service experience to suit their own wants, needs, and context, effectively makes them an active and influential participant in the world of business.

The redistribution of power is challenging for many business leaders and owners, which is why adoption of co-creation models and processes in traditionally more conservative and hierarchical organizations has been slow, exposing those organizations to further disruption from more innovative companies.

THE STORY

As we take up Richard's story once again, note how he responded to his situation by using the think tank/brainstorm approach. He was also creative in how he engaged his stakeholders, which helped him rebuild confidence among skeptical franchisees.

After Richard's meeting with his key players, the large audience of people were still a little tense, but they were much more receptive to what he was about to say. His key stakeholders were clearly communicating their satisfaction with the direction they had agreed on.

The next part of his strategy was his keynote presentation to the entire organization. It had to be one of the best speeches of his career. He spoke for an hour. **He started by falling on his sword. "I failed you," he told them.** "I didn't do a good job of telling you how hard this would be. That was complicated by the fact that it was harder than I even thought it would be." He admitted that the platform was not what he wanted or what he had hoped for.

Then he described the events of that morning in some detail. He told them how the room was literally wallpapered with dozens of flip chart pages, and each page listed dozens of issues that the key stakeholders (their peers) were upset about.

He talked about the formation of the project board and introduced the board members who were already selected, having them stand up in the audience. He explained the plan they had created in more detail and discussed how it would be a completely co-creative process, with qualified stakeholders leading and managing the project. He ended his presentation about the platform by saying:

"EGBOK. Everything's Going to Be OK. Not because I say it will—but because we are doing the hard work to make this vision become a reality. I stand here with people who know how to work hard. I stand here with people who are committed to this company. I stand here with people who are committed to what we are doing. I stand here with people who have a shared vision of where we are going. And that's why I say—Everything's Going to Be OK. We are on the precipice of change, and we have the chance to lock in our position as the world's most successful organization in our field for the next decade and beyond. **Someday, someone is going to write about this project in a book** as an example of what people can do to work together and co-create a solution to a critical need. This platform will be a game changer for our organization. We will do this by working together to create something amazing that works for all of us.

"That is our mantra. That is our vision. That is our future. One platform.

"Everything's Going to be OK."

He had his staff go up and down the aisles and pass out more EGBOK buttons as he stepped offstage to a roaring crowd.

Then came the pièce de résistance of his plan: He had a singer come onstage and perform a special EGBOK song. As crazy as it sounds, it went over amazingly well. The audience loved it and even sang along: "Everything's Going to Be OK, Everything's Going to Be OK..."

The final piece of Richard's plan was to meet with the conference attendees in small groups over the next four days. In those meetings, he planned to do a deep dive on the co-creation of the platform and continue to soothe everyone's nerves about the project. One of those groups was the newly formed project board—the heart of the co-creative process that lay ahead.

The bloodbath that had resulted from the previous attempt to integrate this platform into the business was high on Richard's mind. He was elated that he had successfully coaxed the organization into moving ahead with a co-creative process that would allow the system to rise from the ashes. But it wasn't going to be easy.

The other side of the problem was that there were still people who wanted the program to meet their needs, not the needs of the entire organization. One of the program testers for the project told Richard, "This project will, by its very nature, enforce one uniform process to be utilized across the entire global enterprise. That will make some stakeholders very unhappy because they like the way they are doing it now—even if it is not the best way to do it globally." Richard understood that **these people were happy in their hole and they didn't want a ladder.** But a uniform franchise process was key to the company's success. Like it or not, they would have to get a ladder and start climbing.

He knew that **co-creation is both a thing of beauty and a muddy mess at the same time.** After the convention, the real work would begin.

Contribution and Selection

Co-creation focuses on two main activities that all stakeholders engage in repeatedly during the process: *contribution* and *selection.*

Contribution means stakeholders are providing ideas, views, and opinions. *Selection* means those ideas are reviewed and filtered: Some are discarded, and some are chosen to move forward with and implement.

For Jerome Conlon, former global head of marketing at Nike and former VP of global branding at Starbucks, the experience of bringing together people from across many different disciplines and having them work together co-creatively was key to Nike's tenfold growth and Starbucks' global expansion during his tenure:

[At Nike], we solved a lot of hard problems, but with friendship, and a culture where people can be loose and relaxed. If you're in a team that is fearful of people saying the wrong thing or offending someone, if you just can't speak your mind or you're not free with your insights, then the team will not flourish. So you have to create conditions where it's OK for people to be foolish from time to time in stating stupid things. And just like a group of college friends, your friends will ridicule you or laugh at you or tease you. And you'll learn your lesson if you do something really stupid, but they won't eject you from the group, and the group dynamic just gets stronger and stronger as time goes on.

Most people want to feel part of a group, they want to be in on things, they want to be learning. If you noticed, I didn't say salary or title. If you create the right group dynamics, where people are learning and growing, and they're part of a group effort, have some wins and some losses, but the bottom line is you're moving forward and you're learning as you're going, then you're in a good place.

Phil Knight [founder of Nike] had me study Disney and the biography of the company, its adventures and misadventures, for insight into what Nike might be able to do. And I did come away from that [with insight]. It was about a three- to four-month process of me reading a dozen books and getting all the annual reports and interviewing a few people at Disney. And I came up with 10 points that Nike could benefit from hearing for its own creative and marketing process.

Starbucks approached co-creation very differently. Starbucks had a design team at the center of the company that was always coming up with new cafe concepts. And they wanted to create the ideal coffeehouse into a rich and layered look because of the role that a coffee shop or a coffeehouse plays in people's lives. And so we studied history, the architecture in Europe, and the role and history of coffee around the world. I was a part of putting that learning together for the group. And at the same time, they had to be modular and have a kit of parts so they could commit bulk orders so we could get the unit cost down. Starbucks had to simultaneously create four different store formats, lift the customer experience, and lower the cost by 22 percent. And they did it through a couple of yearlong design exercises at the center of the company.

Just south of Seattle, in the 11-story brick monstrosity, one of the largest buildings in the country square-footage-wise, we had a section on one of the floors that was set for building full-scale models of what these coffeehouses of the future were going to look like. And it was all under the direction of an award-winning architect named Wright Massey. Disney had hired Wright Massey from an architecture firm in New York in the early 1990s. He was brought out from New York to the Disney headquarters in Burbank. And they instilled the mission in Wright Massey's mind: Retail as entertainment. How do we design a retail store to echo the Disney entertainment themes? And so he designed the first retail as entertainment store in America. It was opened in the Glendale Galleria mall in Glendale, California, and it was a resounding success. As a result, Disney started building out these Disney stores. And Howard Schultz [CEO of Starbucks] took notice of that and recruited Wright Massey away from Disney to bring him to Seattle. And when I was hired away from Nike to go to Starbucks, I was thrown together with Wright. He has five college degrees. He has an MBA, and he's a fine artist. He's an illustrator like Tinker Hatfield [Nike's legendary sneaker designer], but he can also break out the specs of a new building down to each nail and nut, and he knows how to negotiate volume discounts, and his knowledge of the creative process in building these stores and lifting the experience was phenomenal.

He created a team around him like Walt Disney did. He had 50 people working on every aspect of design, from wall murals to designing light fixtures to designing counters and displays and seating areas, fireplaces and water features, and how the lighting in the store could be utilized in different ways.

We did a full cultural anthropology on coffee. Coffee in America hadn't been reinvented in over 50 years when Starbucks came along. Coffee got its start in Arabia and has been around for about 600 years, but it's been in Europe for about 500 years. It slowly moved from Austria to France and Italy. The president of the leading Italian coffee brand came to Starbucks to visit with Howard Schultz when I was present. We took him through our R&D labs to show him what we were doing with all the varietals and blends. We took him through the store, the new Wright Massey-designed cafés of the future. And we ended with the coffee tasting room, where we had 40 different varieties that were being tasted. Howard Schultz knew that coffee could be taken further. So there's a lesson in business model reinvention right there, and if you're a knowledge worker, a mind worker in any modern society anywhere in the world, then you know that a really good cup of coffee can make a tremendous difference in your day.

Anyway, after the Italian gentleman experienced all that, he said, "I came over here thinking that we were way more experienced and sophisticated. Now that I've been through your operation and see what you're doing, I've got to take it back. What you're doing is way more sophisticated than anything that we could even envision."

Not everyone needs to roll back their value proposition to the origin of their market, like Starbucks did with coffee. But as the above example shows, unearthing the depth of contribution of those who came before you allows you to appreciate that contribution and then discover during the selection process what remains to be tried. When you identify what hasn't been done but is desired by the customer base, you can create a new market. That is what Starbucks achieved.

You must lay a foundation that ensures the co-creative process can be a valuable and agreeable experience for everyone involved. Take time from the outset to get clarity about what you are doing, where you are hoping to go, and how you intend to get there. In short, analyze your plan along the "The Four Knows" model: Does it generate a *mutually desired outcome (the right focus)* and deploy a solid implementation strategy that includes an *underlying process (the right process), open communication (the right communication),* and *solid execution (the right execution)?*

These steps are an integral part of the co-creative process and are part of why we saw a need for this book. In our survey, many people demonstrated how unstructured and convoluted co-creative processes can lead to frustrating, weak results. This survey respondent shared their story:

> In a previous job, I had started writing a region-specific newsletter for my six-state region and 600-plus employees. My boss asked me to work with the other five regional managers to help them each develop their own newsletter. It was a mess...half of the group abdicated responsibility and dumped it on the other three (including me), who couldn't agree on a layout. Employees started asking to not have it sent anymore, and the whole thing fell flat and was discontinued entirely.

Benefits of Having a Process

Whenever novel ideas and perspectives are generated, limiting beliefs and personal biases can also surface, hampering the contribution and selection process. Carefully monitor these during the empowerment and execution phase to avoid diluting the power of co-creation during implementation and failing to achieve the mutually desired outcome.

Humans are creatures of habit, and any kind of creation can be messy. Watch children play in the sand on the beach or finger-paint in your living room. We are born to create, but any time you leave the well-trodden path there will be plenty of new trampled foliage all over the ground.

Co-creation is no different. It is a "transparent process of value creation... with end users playing a central role," according to authors Stefanie Jansen and Maarten Pieters in *The 7 Principles of Complete Co-Creation*. Sparks can fly and opinions can clash when you first start down this path. People's unexpressed brilliance can surface, along with their repressed prejudices, fears, strong opinions, and narrow, limited views.

Gathering people into a congruent process, especially when you want to make sure everyone gets to have input, can get complicated. Unless everyone has agreed in advance on an effective process, co-creation gets tiresome: One survey respondent said, "we were trying to make enormous decisions by consensus across an extremely diverse group of stakeholders. Decisions by consensus would be delayed month after month, and as the time dragged on, it exacerbated issues that would have otherwise been simple to deal with."

To keep moving toward the mutually desired outcome, a strong process with clear parameters, sequential steps, and defined stages helps you drive the co-creation forward with some observable predictability. You only have three choices, for example, on how you want to exercise a decision-making process within your co-creation team: authority, majority, and consensus. (We'll discuss these in more detail in Chapter 8.) Some other important benefits of having a process are:

- **You stay organized.** A clear process helps you get and stay organized. It allows you to track your progress and helps you not lose sight of your motivation or the value that is generated with a co-creation approach. One survey respondent reported:

  When I worked in community leadership, several community centers tried to come together to create a service that would make it easier for the general public to use one membership across all community centers in the city. Previously, each center had had its own rates and membership structure. It was a nightmare from the beginning. Every center served a different type of population and dug in their heels when it came to finding a middle ground to unify this service into a single streamlined offering. We are talking about years of debate, years of wasted time and effort, angry stakeholders, and mediation. I was relieved to move to another city and be done with it! I feel as if this exercise didn't work because there were no initial parameters placed on participation.

- It is critical to get and stay organized for people not to experience confusion and frustration about the process.

- It also helps you make sure that as many views and voices as possible are being heard, considered, and integrated into your mutually desired outcome with greater transparency and higher perceived impartiality.

- **You stay on track.** Co-creation can take people out of their comfort zone and can also generate large amounts of new input and information. Working with a strong process helps everyone stay focused.

- **You don't waste time.** It is easy to get caught up in the contribution stage of the co-creative process. Once you start asking people for their ideas, you might be surprised just how many they have to offer. The risk is that you may end up generating countless new ideas but never doing anything with them because no one condenses the information and begins to implement it.

  ▶ It seems ideas are infinite, yet most of them are never implemented. Implementation can be difficult and often requires focus, determination, and perseverance. Choosing a process that not only helps you generate lots of new ideas and select the best ones but also helps you devise a focused plan for implementation and continuous action can save you a great deal of time and wasted effort.

- **You deliver predictable results.** A basic process with an identifiable, step-by-step progression will provide you with *a system* to deliver recurring and predictable outcomes.

As we mentioned at the beginning of the chapter, people have historically settled near rivers—and in part that's because they allow you to predict with some accuracy how long it will take you to grow your fields or get your shipments to port.

When you work with specific processes of co-creation in business you will see that following recurring processes can deliver replicable experiences and predictably consistent positive results for you, your team, and your organization.

Determine Roles and Responsibilities

By deciding on a process, you are further along than most in your co-creation journey. Now you have to work on how to effectively make use of it.

A strong underlying support system will allow your co-creative project to thrive. It starts by getting clear on who will do what by when. Take the time to identify which roles you will need to fill, and make sure you appoint and empower people to execute those specific roles and responsibilities. Here are some possible roles to consider:

- **Facilitator:** The responsibility of the facilitator is to lead the contribution and selection process and facilitate co-creation in a way that allows everyone to contribute on some level. Important tasks include making sure people understand what stage of the process they are in and keeping the process moving forward within the constraints of the agreed-upon guidelines.

- **Notetaker:** The responsibility of the notetaker is to record the contributions made by people participating in the co-creative process. Sometimes this task can be automated with the help of technology (GroupMap, WiseMapping, Stormz, etc.), and participants can enter their contributions on their own. It is important to make certain that nothing gets lost, as that would frustrate contributors and potentially undermine the co-creative process.

- **Evaluator:** The responsibility of the evaluator is to review the gathered ideas and suggestions and select the most promising ones for the project. They report back to the community with the results. This process can be democratized through voting.

- **Implementer:** The Implementer is charged with the implementation of the decisions that are taken as part of co-creation. They must execute or oversee the execution of actionable tasks and will report back to the community on progress.

- **Assessor:** The responsibility of the assessor is to assess the results of the project. They review the level of success and the achieved project milestones and report back. Based on that review, everyone knows what progress has been made and if things are on track or have to be adjusted.

Why You Need Clear Roles and Responsibilities

Clearly defined roles and responsibilities are essential if you want to keep a co-creative process moving forward and avoid major roadblocks.

Thirty-six percent of those taking part in our survey reported *lack of agreement on who makes the final decision* as one of the major drawbacks to co-creation.

When you take the time to identify who is responsible for what, everyone knows who to look to when it comes to completing various stages of the process. This helps avoid *lack of accountability,* which more than 30 percent of people in our survey described as a main drawback and major frustration in co-creation.

Creating clear roles and responsibilities boils down to how leaders focus on generating clarity around everyone's expectations early on in the process. Without such clarity, people will disengage. Like one survey responder reported: "Always the same tune; different key, different beat, but same song. No clarity, no key leader, no roles, no accountability, just egos. Yuk!" Therefore, you have to establish and assign clear roles and responsibilities right out of the gate.

Here is a simple four-step outline of how to start:

1. Begin by writing down what roles and responsibilities you will need for your co-creation project.

2. Identify people who could serve in a particular role and who possess some social capital of trust and integrity within the community.

3. Go over the specific responsibilities of each role and think about the timelines and commitments you wish to associate with each one.

4. Once you have those things written down, review them with the people you wish to invite or appoint to take on the specific roles. Make sure they sign off on what they commit to do.

Establish Governance

Every co-creative process takes place within a community, even if that community is small. Since co-creation is a process by which people work together, it is by its very nature a communal process. Communities, in business and in life, organize themselves around shared origins, interests, and objectives. These can be organized further into shared principles, values, purpose, mission, vision, strategies, tactics, tasks, and metrics of success. Maintaining awareness and stewardship of all these elements is part of good governance.

The person or persons who start a business or a co-creative process often also are the ones whose governance most strongly affects the culture of that organization or project.

Co-creation can bring to the surface important aspects that the initiator or founders may have overlooked. While people assemble themselves most often around leaders with whom they share aspects of governance, leaders are often surprised at the nuanced and diverse sentiments and perspectives that arise during co-creation. Forty-six percent of people report a shared feeling of ownership as a top benefit of co-creation; an opportunity thus exists for leaders to induct more people into their organization's culture by engaging them in co-creation.

If you can, to support your co-creation and overall success, publicize your governance so everyone involved in the co-creative process knows and understands what is driving your decision making and co-creation at a deeper level. That allows them to operate from a greater shared meaning than just what is available during daily interactions and will make their contribution much more valuable and actionable within the context of what you are hoping to mutually achieve.

You can apply the above to each of the five types of co-creation we mention throughout this book. Whether you are choosing think tank/brainstorm, crowdsource, open source, mass customization, or user-generated content as your track to a mutually desired outcome, your co-creative process should still have a defined scope, set boundaries, sequencing, clear roles and responsibilities, and a transparent governance structure.

Unconscious Bias

Co-creation is most limited by our lack of awareness of and appreciation for *unconscious bias*. In general, we don't know what we don't know, and what we don't know or what we think we know when we don't can be the source of much ignorance and confusion. It is an implicit bias, blindness, or skewed view and set of prejudices of which the person themselves is unaware, but which nevertheless influence every perspective they hold and every decision they make.

As a co-creator, it is your job to bring your own unconscious bias to the surface, making it conscious, so that its influence on successful co-creation can be minimized or eliminated.

Unconscious bias exists because of gender, age, race, religion, hierarchy, and many other individual differences. It can be the result of your upbringing and education or the cultural environment in which you live and work. It affects your vantage point for perspectives on problems, as well as your preferred pathway to solutions.

Different genders, for example, often have very different ways of solving problems. Some people may approach problems as more transactional and needing to be fixed, while others may view them as more relational, needing to be understood and talked through.

The book *Business Networking and Sex (not what you think)* argues *that the exception becomes the perception.* This means that, in general, we form strong biases around gender based on those individuals who stand out in contrast. It is not the average man who informs our image of what men are like, but those men who stand out for their nonaverage, even extreme behavior. And it is not the majority of women who form our perception of what women are like, but the women who stand out thanks to their unique and sometimes excessive behavior. That is how stereotypes are created: by making assumptions about noticeable, exceptional behavior that stands out and applying them to a larger group of people to whom, in general, the stereotype does not apply.

Unconscious bias exists in all areas of daily life. People from different cultural or socioeconomic backgrounds may see the world through very different lenses and may seek divergent solutions to similar problems.

People from different levels within an organization may have contrasting perspectives and ideas about why a problem exists or how it can best be solved.

Manage Unconscious Bias

Unconscious bias can skew or hamper the results of your co-creation, so it is important to pay attention to it. In a company, for example, listening only to management and leadership and not to the people on the floor or on the front lines can be a fatal mistake. Not embracing changing market realities or the needs and preferences of different generations of customers or the workforce can cost a business dearly.

Operating from a limited and biased perspective in a fast-changing, competitive landscape can cost an organization access to the most innovative and high-performing employees, and it can quickly make a business irrelevant in the 21st century, where adaptiveness is key for an organization to survive, let alone thrive.

Unconscious bias is a risk that organizations should be committed to eliminating or reducing as much as possible. There are numerous intelligent approaches for exposing and reducing unconscious bias (which are beyond the scope of this book): counter stereotype training, negation training, perspective taking, meditation, and implicit bias training. These are all effective tools that have shown results, according to Francesca Gino and Katherine Coffman in their 2021 article "Unconscious Bias Training That Works" for the *Harvard Business Review.*

Jon Berghoff, founder of Xchange Approach, a meeting facilitation company, shared with us the importance of equal voices for effective co-creation:

> While most co-creative conversations will have several steps, the first step should always be an invitation for voices to equally contribute to the conversation at hand. Research on psychological safety suggests that without voices being given an equal invitation to share, a process will undermine the safety of the

participants before it ever gets off the ground. And without safety, groups will never make it through the necessary tensions of a co-creative process. A conscious facilitator has a continuous eye on which voices are contributing, which ones aren't, and will design for this versus leave it to chance.

Unconsciously privileging some voices over others will undermine co-creation. By being aware of and managing your unconscious bias, you can reduce its limiting and harmful effects on your co-creative process.

Set Context

When planning and implementing co-creation, put some effort early into establishing context, as one survey respondent recommended:

> I have found the best way to develop a process that will ulti-mately be successful is to get the team involved in the beginning, or what I call the "Understanding the Problem" phase. Once everyone agrees that there is a problem and what we are trying to avoid in the future (end goal), we then brainstorm, asking each team member to come up with a possible solution, including the steps required to complete the issue at hand.

The clearer people feel about what they are doing (as well as when, where, why, and how), the easier co-creation will be.

Setting context is critical to achieving clarity. Make the context spe-cific enough to not get lost or overwhelmed. A more specific context helps everyone stay focused, makes it easier for them to contribute, and keeps their contributions more valuable and precise. In our experience, there are recurring types of co-creative contexts: strategic, tactical, and situational, to name just three. Each of these contexts has its own time and place in which it tends to arise.

Strategic Context

Where do we want to end up? Start with the end in mind.

Strategic context arises when a business, organization, or group needs to make decisions about its long-term direction and commitments. Strategic co-creation might not be ongoing but something that your organization has to engage in several times a year.

Tactical Context

How are we going to get there?

Tactical context is important when you must decide how you are going to proceed. What actions are you going to take to arrive at your destination, and how will you perform those actions?

Situational Context

What, when, where, why, and who?

Situational context is reactionary; it matters most when you have to adapt to the situation at hand. It requires you to be aware of the demands of each unique situation and decide how to best respond to it. In contrast to strategic and tactical contexts, which allow you to think ahead and plan your course of action, situational context means acting with a great deal of responsiveness and adaptability—and, ideally, in alignment with your previously established strategic and tactical decisions.

Good leaders develop contextual intelligence—capably discerning the varying contexts—and are good facilitators. They understand the context of their situation from a long-term and short-term perspective. This understanding can take time to develop, so leaders are willing to put in the time to think things through whenever possible. A leader also understands the limits of their knowledge and adapts that knowledge to different environments. Good leadership is about making the best possible match between their needs and the available resources, in light of the vision, mission, strategy, and goals.

Even once you have developed your contextual intelligence to deal with challenges, you cannot anticipate all the potential challenges that may come your way. Good leaders therefore build their capacity to adapt as a core competency. And since you cannot plan for every unexpected situation, simply do your best, be flexible, and expect that "what cannot go wrong will go wrong."

Conclusion

When co-creation goes wrong, it can go very wrong. You can compare it to someone trying to put a piece of furniture together or running a piece of expensive machinery without taking the time to read the instructions.

Getting clear on the right process and working through the kind of process you would like to use in your endeavor isn't just recommended as far as we're concerned: It is mandatory. A co-creative process without clear steps, roles and responsibilities, or good governance can be unnecessarily frustrating for everyone—and burn bridges. You are about to bring your most important stakeholders together to help you create massive value. Why would you leave the outcome to chance when you have everything you need to make it a well-organized, streamlined, and enjoyable experience for all involved by investing early in setting up a good process? The success or failure of your next co-creation is in your hands.

CHAPTER 7

The Third Know:
The Right Communication

Many business professionals recognize the importance of communication in co-creation projects. In our survey, we asked respondents to choose up to seven drawbacks to co-developing a product, service, or idea. "Poor communication" ranked third, with 40.70 percent of people identifying it as a disadvantage to co-creative work. ("Personality conflicts," with 58.25 percent, and "dealing with egos," with 57.33 percent, came in first and second.)

Effective communication in *any* organization is crucial, but it is even more important for co-creation. Perhaps one of our survey respondents said it best: "When there is not clear communication (from above to below and the other way around), the whole thing might collapse!" For co-creation to succeed, leaders must ensure there is a process for communicating transparently and with all stakeholders. *Right communication* in the Co-Creation Model also means that value is being created along every step of the way—and trust among stakeholders is reaffirmed as well. See Figure 7.1 below.

Communication in a Co-Creative Environment

Let's start with the basics. What is communication, and how do we communicate effectively in conversation? Much of the co-creative process

Figure 7.1 Co-Creation Model: The Right Communication

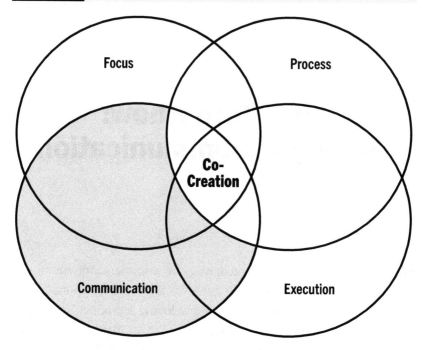

requires talking to one another, so stakeholders in a co-creative endeavor must learn to communicate in a way that adds value.

Communication is *what is heard*. It is not *what is said*. If you are trying to communicate an important message to your co-creation team, you must have the self-awareness to recognize when what you are *saying* does not align with what they are *hearing*, and then adjust accordingly. This should also prompt you to reflect on what makes good conversation, so everyone in your organization can be heard.

Communication is *what is heard.* It is not *what is said.*

We can gain insight from the original meaning of the word conversation, which goes back to Latin via 14th-century French: "The act of living with," "Living together, having dealings with others," and the "manner of conducting oneself in the world." The popular meaning of the word has since evolved into its main modern usage of "talking." There is much to be learned about conversation by connecting to the original sense.

When having a conversation, we are in a state of active exchange that begins with being together. We can't exchange something with someone who's not present. We can talk to them, we can talk at them, but we can't have a conversation.

In contrast, talking is a self-referential activity. We talk because we have something to say. We often find out afterward that no one was listening, or if they were, they didn't understand us.

Does the value of a precious thing lie in throwing it away? Of course not. The value of talking lies not in what is being said but entirely in what is being heard. We don't communicate to be ignored, misinterpreted, or misunderstood. We give to be received.

We recommend you reevaluate your conversation style based on the following five steps. You might find that valuable doors open and a more mindful form of conversation begins to appear as well.

1. **Be present.** The root word *con-* means "together with." If you want to have a *con*versation, be fiercely present. Nothing can be exchanged if you are not here, mentally as well as physically, and the value of a conversation lies in what both participants give.

2. **Think before you speak.** Take the time you need to craft your language carefully. It doesn't matter how quickly or how slowly you respond; what matters is how much value is in your reply. There is pleasure in both quick wit and deliberate reasoning. But if there is no value in your words, everyone will end the conversation as soon as they can get away.

3. **Become hearable.** Hearability—the quality of a message to be heard, absorbed, and understood—is the determinant of great conversation. We love it when we are affected by what we hear and respond when words move us. If your words have no hearability, don't blame your audience; engage it.

4. **Be relational before being transactional.** Take time to develop the relational aspect of the conversation without focusing solely on what you can get out of it. You're building a human connection through which you will be able to exchange ideas, experiences and

insights. The better the connection, and the more open people are, the more value you can exchange. Trust builds that connection and opening; so does being heard. If you have a lot to say or ask for, make sure the connection and relational opening of your conversation can handle what you are asking for and intend to communicate. Emotional intelligence is an integral piece of this element. **Participants need to be cognizant of the emotional investments that some parties have to the position they are espousing.**

5. **Enjoy yourself and let go.** A real exchange happens when all sides are enriched. Focus on enjoying yourself for the entire conversation—not just when you got what you came for or said your piece. You don't sing just to get to the end of the song or live to get to the end of life. Enjoyment is a choice—a mindful one at that—and part of the art of conversation. Then, when you're done, let it go.

When people use this approach to conversation while leading or working on a co-creation team, meetings tend to be a lively exchange of value that advances the co-creation project, rather than the dreadful bores that are the subject of memes and jokes.

Methods of Communication

How you communicate is as important as *what* you communicate. People have different learning styles, and different styles of communication resonate with some people more than others. Communicate in a variety of ways. You'll find that some people like to experience a live event, while others will want memos, a slide deck, or interactive webinars. Providing a mix of methodologies enables you to connect with people in their preferred manner. Be open to change, and consider adding new methods of communication when they come along.

Beyond using diverse methods, you must also consider who you are communicating with and adapt your style accordingly. For anyone implementing changes or who is "on the ground," detailed information is warranted. Likewise, for anything complicated, communicating in detail is important.

That doesn't mean that everyone wants highly detailed information, however. Executives and entrepreneurs will likely prefer a different approach. People in these roles tend to appreciate summarized information and even bulleted lists. Sending a lengthy email to an executive might result in no response or a "TL;DR" reply—"too long; didn't read."

Ivan

I recall a critical learning moment in my academic career as a graduate student when a professor assigned our class to write a 10-page paper. We turned in our papers at the beginning of class, and by the end of class the professor had already returned them with "minor feedback": He told us that next week, we had to cover the same material, but in only five pages. We found this frustrating but as told, a week later, we had pruned our papers to half their size and turned them in. Again, our professor returned them by the end of class, now telling us to reduce them to two pages each, while not losing any important meaning. Now we were really confused and annoyed but again, we did as we were told. A week later, the professor told us to write a one-page executive summary for the full 10-page report we had originally handed in. The ordeal was incredibly frustrating at the time, but in the end, it was also one of the most valuable learning exercises I have ever completed. The professor had us turn in the 10 page paper once again but this time it was with the one page executive summary on the front. The importance of being able to communicate key information succinctly can hardly be overstated.

When communicating in writing, whatever the form, be clear, concise, and thoughtful. Do not write emails as a stream of consciousness or send a document in such a hurry that it is incomprehensible. Leave emotion out of your writing.

In turn, when reading other people's writing, be open to new ideas and assume good intent. Nothing is gained from becoming angry over an email, written feedback, or policy changes. Differences in opinion in co-creative endeavors is where the magic can happen. Read to learn, and then respond—either in writing or in conversation.

Shared Vocabulary

When we hear two people having a conversation in a language we don't know, we can often pick up on nonverbal communication: whether they are happy, angry, agitated, or exhausted. We can read their mood by their gestures, tone, and even the volume of their voice. What we are missing, however, is *meaning*. What are they laughing about? What are they fighting over? Without a shared vocabulary, we might be able to play along with their conversation for a bit—maybe offering a small smile from across the room when they laugh and look our way—but we will never know what it was about. We won't ever be able to join their conversation in a meaningful way that adds value.

A lack of understanding also occurs when co-creative teams do not share a common vocabulary, even if they speak the same language. When this happens, people talk past each other—maybe nodding or shaking their head when they sense it's warranted—without ever understanding what the other people have to say.

For this reason, creating a shared vocabulary, or even a project glossary, at the outset of a co-creation project is a useful step to reduce miscommunication and increase the exchange of value in every conversation.

Communication, Stakeholders, and the Five Types of Co-Creation

Each of the five types of co-creation might have different stakeholders involved at different stages of the process, serving various roles. Some teams might have more than 100 people involved total, but only 50 at any given time. Smaller teams might have three committed members throughout the entire co-creative process.

Below are examples of how stakeholders might be engaged differently depending on the type of co-creation an organization uses. These are only examples to help you imagine what each type of co-creation might look like in practice and how the right communication is crucial for success.

Think Tank/Brainstorm

As we discussed in Chapter 2, in this type, stakeholders involved with in-person think tanks and brainstorming come together to develop a new solution, product, or service.

Depending on the goal, company founders and executives might start by engaging end users and having focus groups clarify where things are going well and where they are not. In this example, project leaders must communicate with focus group leaders to ensure they are asking the right questions and facilitating the discussion to elicit maximum input from potential end users. Communication must be open, honest, and transparent to make sure end users are being equally transparent with their feedback.

Crowdsource

One of the best-known crowdsourcing and mass collaboration organizations is Wikipedia. The nonprofit organization, whose online encyclopedia is written and maintained by volunteers, is committed to its mission to provide open access information without advertisements. Crowdsourcing and mass collaboration has expanded greatly over the previous two decades; now it is common to use apps that solicit users' input. Two examples are Waze (which crowdsources traffic reports to find you the best route) and Zooniverse (a web portal that relies on volunteers to assist professional researchers).

For these types of organizations, clear communication with the end users, who both consume and contribute to content, is crucial—they need to know their role (typically as volunteers) and how the organization will use the information they submit. With a clear process in place, crowdsourcers will willingly update encyclopedia entries, report traffic accidents, and contribute to scientific discoveries and publications.

Open Source

Through this type of co-creation, stakeholders often feel a sense of shared ownership and shared resources. Open source innovation relies on technology. Common successful open source examples, as we discussed in Chapter 2, include the Linux family of operating systems and VLC Media Player.

Pitfalls can abound when the right communication is lacking. ResearchGate, an open access platform aimed at sharing academic research, experienced significant bumps along the way of its startup journey. Before course-correcting, it was criticized for practices tied, in part, to poor communication. ResearchGate had a habit of emailing invitations to join the site to authors of scientific articles, which appeared to come from the recipient's coauthor. Until ResearchGate changed its email practices, some members of the academic community distrusted them. Today, while still facing some legal challenges to its research sharing model, it is perhaps the best-known open access social network among academics.

Pitfalls can abound when the right communication is lacking.

Mass Customization

Shutterfly, a company known for mass customization of digital images, was a pioneer of this type of co-creation. A 2009 Forbes interview with the former CEO of Shutterfly, Jeff Housenbold, revealed the importance of communication with all stakeholders in the scaling of Shutterfly. Housenbold discussed his communications with the board of directors, how he gained buy-in from them for his growth plan, and how the company closely communicated with vendors Xerox and Hewlett-Packard so it could "drive innovation and drive price lower." Moreover, he stated, "Involving the consumer in the whole process is key to success." Examples like this highlight how communicating with all stakeholders, especially while scaling, is crucial for success.

User-Generated Content

YouTube might be the first company that comes to mind when thinking about co-creation through user-generated content (UGC). UGC relies on the internet for widespread sharing of content through social media platforms like Twitter, review sites like Yelp, and sites for endless conversations like Reddit.

As our survey revealed, people view access to shared resources as a key benefit of co-creation. It is thanks to UGC that we can look up a question on the internet and get thousands of hits. Collectively, as individuals and groups, we have built the largest UGC undertaking of all time: the ever-growing body of knowledge that is the internet.

Communicating with consumers can take many forms for companies using this type of co-creation, with an important one being company policies and legal terms. A platform can lose trust with its consumers if they find out their information is being sold or used in a way they were unaware of. Moreover, consumers can disengage with a site if it doesn't clearly communicate its policies. More and more social platforms are being launched, with varying success, in response to a perceived censoring that can sometimes happen when a platform bans a person's account for violating policies that perhaps the consumer did not even know existed.

Regardless of *what* type of co-creation you have selected and who the stakeholders are—developers, end users, vendors, investors, senior leaders, etc.—everyone must communicate openly and honestly. Open communication is crucial to growth, as the following survey respondent emphasizes: "In companies where ideas are freely shared, a tremendous amount of growth happens. I have been at companies where the people in charge did not want to hear any ideas that weren't their own, so no growth happens there."

The Risks of Poor Communication

As consumers, we've all encountered organizations with poor communication: a restaurant that serves us ravioli when we ordered lasagna, the mechanic who changes our oil when we only wanted a car inspection, or the supposedly ‹indestructible› tablet protector that breaks the first time your toddler drops your device. Each of these experiences are the result of poor communication: the end users are dissatisfied and will likely not buy from the company again.

Beware of red flags that signal poor communication. In organizations with poor communication, people often do not abide by the old maxim of "You have two ears and one mouth; use them proportionally." Some talk a lot but don't listen. Excessive noise from some stakeholders can lead to insufficient input from the rest. In other words, the organization might have plenty of information but very little wisdom.

Poor leadership, is, of course, linked to poor communication. When leaders communicate poorly, they might not ensure progress updates are being shared, they might not share a written outline of the project with all stakeholders, and they might not even communicate at all—orally, in writing, or even through recorded video updates—due to the organizational hierarchy.

This type of communication will lead to project failure, poor morale, and skepticism among stakeholders regarding the value of co-creation.

Communication Saturation

When there is a situation like this within an organization, we recommend a strategy we call *communication saturation.* Co-creation will fail when trust breaks down or when stakeholders become skeptical or fearful of the process.

At this point, the leader must intervene and correct course by communicating **to such an extent that it is impossible for any stakeholder to say they were uninformed,** didn't know about something, or didn't have an opportunity to voice their concern. That's communication saturation.

The specifics might be different depending on the stakeholders involved, the type of co-creation model, and the product or service. Here are a handful of examples:

- Holding weekly (or daily) meetings for all stakeholders, either in person or virtually
- Sending weekly progress reports
- Maintaining an open-door policy to facilitate transparency

All these steps help make the process of co-creation more transparent. Once stakeholders have clarity regarding the process and progress, confusion dissipates. As a leader, you will know you've reached communication saturation when fewer people are complaining, asking questions, or showing up to live events.

You can then scale down the communication saturation strategy once the stakeholders' questions have been answered and anxieties have been calmed. Frequent, clear, and authentic communication must remain throughout the co-creative process.

THE STORY

We pick up our story at the point when Richard was recognizing the challenges his project would face because of poor communication within his organization and the steps he took to resolve the issues. You'll see our strategy of communication saturation in action; as Richard used this approach, he worked diligently to shepherd everyone toward one consistent solution and vision rather than the many competing solutions they had created in the past.

The next challenge, Richard understood, was that **poor communication at all levels of the project would create major problems for the co-creative process.** Things would fall apart quickly unless there was almost complete transparency and regular communication throughout the project. He began by setting expectations. He released a communication plan to all the key stakeholders for them to review and comment on. This set the baseline for what people could expect.

There had to be regular communications to help manage the message and ensure that his stakeholders felt they were being kept appropriately informed. **His primary strategy was communication saturation,** so that people would find it almost impossible to say they "didn't know what was going on" in the project. He scheduled weekly global webinars (at different times of the day) open to all stakeholders to update them on the platform's development. At these webinars, he brought in key people in the co-creative process to talk about the project and answer questions. At first, there was massive attendance, a fair amount of anxiety, and many questions. But something interesting happened—as the weeks went by, fewer people came to the webinars and fewer questions were asked. Most notably, the anxiety faded, with only sporadic flare-ups. Regular, transparent communication led directly to less conflict.

He called his communication strategy "multifold" honesty, meaning that it needed to be layered into virtually every element of the project. It was complex, because it involved being transparent and honest while also being relevant and appropriate. For example, he recognized that the team should share relevant staffing issues, but they couldn't broadly discuss confidential HR matters relating to staff. Multifold honesty requires transparency, clarity, and discernment.

In addition, he regularly sent out email summaries of the work they were doing—including the budget and expenditures in many of them. The franchisees were expected to financially contribute to the project when it was completed, and Richard believed it was critical for the project's finances to be transparent, so they would understand the extent of the work.

Another benefit of co-creation that Richard discovered related to the **stronger relationships** that were developed across the company. **The process of iterative improvement through co-creation requires a close working relationship between all parties.** That had many positive side effects on the people, the project, and the organization.

Richard knew that some people wouldn't pull their weight, but he lost more sleep over the people he kept than the ones he let go. When he saw someone who wasn't doing their share of the work, he removed them from the project and put someone else in that person's place. If they were an employee, they wouldn't necessarily be fired, but the project was too important for mediocre work. If they were a stakeholder, they were invited to step down (which, interestingly, almost everyone was willing to do). This experience reminded Richard that when you open the door for nonperformers, they are generally willing and often even happy to walk through it.

While a lack of commitment to the project was not acceptable, disagreements were welcome. Co-creation can't take place without talking through disagreements. For effective communication, they had to be tempered with professionalism. The key was understanding that **you can disagree while still being polite.** This wasn't always practiced, but it was generally sought.

One of the significant benefits that Richard observed was how **people encountered areas of the business that were new to them**. It was like the old parable of the blind men touching an elephant. Each felt a different part of the elephant and said it was a snake, or a tree trunk, or a wall, or a rope. They didn't realize they were all touching the same animal. **Co-creation gave the people working on the project a more complete vision of the entire organization**—they could see the whole elephant, as it were. They realized the size and scope of the project, and, more important, they began to understand the organization as a whole much better.

One area that was a potential challenge for Richard was the **lack of agreement** regarding various aspects of the co-creative process, at all levels of the project. He feared this would exacerbate personality conflicts. This is why finding leaders capable of mediating differences with diplomacy was critical to his plan. In a sense, the lack of agreement on issues had a benefit. It would help to ensure that they would not fall into a "groupthink" mentality.

Groupthink is a sociological phenomenon where people strive for consensus within a group instead of hashing out opposing opinions productively. Oftentimes people will set aside their own personal beliefs or simply endorse the opinion of the rest of the group. This term was first used in 1972 by social psychologist Irving Janis, who diagnosed it as a previously unknown syndrome that he believed was interfering with people's ability to make good decisions within group settings.

But to Richard, conflict was good. It allowed people to brainstorm solutions. People didn't need to go into a discussion "in agreement." Room for disagreement was essential, but disagreement couldn't get in the way of effective co-creation. He created a key performance indicator matrix that groups could use in debates, which served as a baseline for discussions and allowed them to decide on the best course of action.

The result of this approach to co-creation was **more empowered teams and a shared sense of ownership** for the project. This process began with the establishment of the project board, which was fully empowered to triage the list of problems from the initial preconference meeting and prioritize everything that was being developed. As a result, that sense of ownership for the project rippled outward through the organization. The "communication saturation" strategy helped keep that sense of empowerment alive within the company. One of the methods used was to have board members (fellow stakeholders) appear on various webinars to talk to all the other stakeholders about the progress of the project. Having the people involved in the co-creative process helped to address the many concerns that almost always arise in a project of this magnitude.

Despite the advantages of the co-creative process, it is not for the faint of heart. Many people in the organization (including Richard) had low frustration tolerance—a tendency to give up on tasks once they began to feel even slightly frustrated. Most participants would learn that they had to put those frustrations aside to achieve their shared vision.

Seven Principles to Achieve the Right Communication

Like Richard, all leaders can create the right communication within their co-creation teams. Here are seven principles to help you achieve it. These principles apply to all five types of co-creation and speak to the utmost importance of both communication and leadership—common themes in our survey results. One respondent plainly stated: "Communication and leadership are vital. The entire team needs to understand what the end goal is, and there has to be a strong leader who respects everyone on the team and who keeps the group focused."

1. **Everyone speaks.** Not everyone is naturally inclined to speak up. Some people are naturally quieter and more introverted, and others are unsure of themselves. They might not feel like they have a voice—or they might have been led to believe in the past that their opinions don't matter.

   This is a problem for co-creation because the only way for the process to work is if everyone speaks. Leaders must ensure that everyone's voice is heard. **Each of us has a unique perspective that the rest need to hear.**

   When leading a session, set expectations to make sure everyone speaks. A survey respondent addressed this aspect of co-creation: "Clear, concise structure needs to be set up and boundaries [made] very clear about what's required of each individual to bring the project to fruition." We are delighted to hear conversation—whether it's agreement or argument, what matters is that everyone is sharing their perspective. Participants should talk everything out and keep talking until everyone has had their say. To help facilitate this process, sometimes we will go around the room and tell each person, "We want to hear what you have to say." When leaders set the expectation that everyone will speak, engagement will naturally increase.

2. **Everyone respects.** Think of this as Brainstorming 101. In co-creative endeavors, everyone must hear everyone else out, respect others' viewpoints, and be open to truly listening to those viewpoints. There are no dumb suggestions. And remember that everyone is there to achieve the mutually desired outcome.

   The challenge with this principle is that some people inherently *don't* respect other perspectives. We have seen incidents where one person complained that another person was allowed to speak at a meeting; the person complaining believed that the other person was not qualified to offer input. It is important to be prepared for this kind of situation and to make sure that all perspectives are respected and heard.

One person we interviewed said that "when this happens, keep going! This is good! It means that everyone is communicating, even if *everyone is not happy about it.*" Despite some stakeholders having narrow viewpoints, co-creation leaders must cultivate an environment where everyone feels safe to express their views.

Disagreement is OK; people can disagree without being disagreeable. By its nature, co-creation is immersed in disagreement.

Disagreement is OK; people can disagree without being disagreeable. By its nature, co-creation is immersed in disagreement.

As entrepreneur and author Seth Godin says, "The hallmark of a resilient, productive and sustainable culture is that disagreements aren't risky." Encourage participants to see things from the other person's viewpoint. When people disagree with an opinion or suggestion, it's valuable to immediately ask, "What do I find good or right about this?" Doing so points everyone toward progress rather than digging in their heels.

Co-creative organizations are inherently inclusive. It's in their best interest to have full participation from all stakeholders, with everyone demonstrating respect toward one another. Leaders can set the example for what is expected in terms of respect.

3. **Everyone is patient.** When does going faster make things slower? When you rush.

   Co-creation takes time, so this principle is about setting expectations regarding timelines. The following is a story from Dr. Emory Cowan, Former President of the Colorado School of Professional Psychology which first appeared in the book *Masters of Networking*:

Many years ago, I bought some peaches at the farmers' market in Atlanta. They were the famous Georgia peaches, grown in orchards in the Fort Valley region and renowned for their sweet, juicy taste and wonderful aroma. I took them home, visions of peach pies and cobblers dancing in my head. We ate some right away; most sat out on the kitchen counter.

One morning I was awakened by the aroma of peaches filling the house. I knew that something would have to be done with them soon or they would spoil. Wine, I thought. Why not make some peach wine? I knew my parents, who lived 15 miles away, had a ceramic crock and an old family recipe for fermenting wine from fruit. I found the crock, cleaned it, and on the way home bought cheesecloth for the top, along with yeast and sugar for the ingredients.

By the time I got home, my excitement over this project was so great that I could almost taste the new wine as I cut up the peaches, added the sugar and yeast, and closed the top with the cheesecloth. **But the process of making wine is slow, and I was impatient.** With the crock safely stashed in the cool basement, I drove home from work each day with growing excitement. I would go immediately to the crock and smell the brew. As the days went by, I became more intent on having the wine ready for consumption. But it was not happening fast enough for me.

So one afternoon, frustrated that it was taking so long, I carried the crock to the kitchen, determined to speed up the process of fermentation. I removed the contents, used a blender to further emulsify the peaches, and added more sugar and yeast. Smug and satisfied, I returned the crock to the basement, and three days later I had—vinegar!

My vinegar-making triumph has become a life-shaping parable for me. When I am tempted to rush [a] process...I am reminded that some things just take time to happen. I am aware that letting my impatience force the process can turn the potential of new wine into vinegar.

Cowan was not unique in his impatience. People are antsy. Everyone wants things *now*.

For co-creation to work, leaders must communicate their expectations about the timeline and motivate stakeholders. We frequently remind our stakeholders that sometimes we ruin things if we speed them up. Offering encouragement can work wonders. Consider phrases like the following, which both motivate and establish an expectation of pacing yourself:

► Take a deep breath.

► This is a marathon, not a sprint.

► We won't get there overnight.

► This will take time.

4. **Everyone is honest.** Lies of omission harm co-creation. So does, for example, letting people learn from the news a breaking story about the organization they work for. Honesty breaks down when people withhold information that is relevant to decision making. In cases like these, "I didn't do anything wrong" is not the same as being right. Communicating without being honest is the enemy of building trust.

Being honest requires tact, respect, and a commitment to avoid deception. Sharing ideas, giving feedback, and all other kinds of communication must be done professionally. (See Principle #2: Everyone respects.)

All stakeholders should ensure that honesty is front and center in all activities. If you are a stakeholder in a co-creative process, be honest with yourself, each team member, your team as a whole, and the overarching purpose of your project.

Be honest with yourself: Never let anyone influence you to think or act in a way that doesn't align with your values or what you know to be true, based on your expertise or perspective.

Be honest with **each team member:** Every stakeholder is there for a reason. Be honest with them in your communications, knowing they have a unique perspective and expertise to contribute.

Be honest with **the team as a whole:** Communicate in a way that is best for the team, and check that what you are communicating is in line with what the team as a whole is setting out to achieve.

Be honest with **the purpose of your project:** Remember that you are working as part of a co-creative team to achieve a mutually desired outcome. Your overarching purpose should drive your actions, and you must maintain integrity to the co-creative process. Be honest when assessing where you started, where you are, and where you hope to end up.

This honesty will help everyone communicate well and work together efficiently. It is especially important the longer the co-creative process endures and the more failures and successes accumulate.

5. **Everyone is transparent.** Transparency is closely linked to honesty. Transparency must be at the core of all co-creative processes. Stakeholders working together toward a common goal must have access to the information they need to reach milestones in the co-creative process. Lack of transparency harms trust and can reduce stakeholders' commitment to the mutually desired outcome.

   However, it can be a touchy subject. A person can disclose more than is healthy, and disclosure can feed into conflict, emotionality, or drama. Problems linked to disclosing salaries come up frequently within organizations—sometimes forcing organizations to reckon with issues of equity and equality.

   Let's use an example about transparency that could come up at home. Let's say you and your family members have decided to always be transparent with one another. There should be no secrets…but would you tell your 5-year-old where you keep the key to the gun safe? No! Of course not. Transparency also requires a responsible degree of discretion.

We recommend a *healthy, pragmatic transparency* that aligns with logic and any legal constraints (e.g., nondisclosure agreements) stakeholders must abide by. Transparency should have a metric. Co-creation leaders need to determine where transparency increases trust and where it diminishes trust.

Transparency in communicating performance expectations can boost the co-creative process and everyone in it. Performance tends to improve when everyone knows the consequences and rewards for their actions. Co-creation leaders can clarify their expectations by using a matrix of actions and results.

If we think of achieving co-creation as a multiplication equation and transparency as one of the variables, it becomes clear that by managing transparency we can influence the quality of the co-creation. With transparency set to zero, co-creation will also fall to zero. Transparency is that important.

Transparency can be facilitated by using tools such as Google Drive and Trello, where stakeholders can see the work being done, when it was done, and the stages of the co-creative process.

6. **Everyone builds safety and trust.** Co-creative organizations must have everyone committed to actively building safety and trust, which are interrelated. In a practical sense, part of creating a safe environment for all stakeholders includes creating a shared language. When trying to co-create, stakeholders need to communicate effectively with one another—a task made easier by having a shared vocabulary. One survey participant wrote, "It is critical to create a common language and 'safe zones' for experimentation." Doing so reinforces the shared mission of the stakeholders.

   On a broader level, safety and trust are also about how people view each other and approach their work. We have found that trust can be an elephant in the room that people struggle to talk about. This is in part because people have different views of what "trust" is and how they approach it.

The most common attitude is that trust is your response to the degree of safety and support in the world around you, and it is earned. "Make it safe for me, and I will trust you."

We call this reactive approach "trust as earned." The problem with this attitude to trust is that it can easily stifle progress. Our environment, be it people or planet, is never quite safe and predictable enough to earn your trust. And, once trust is lost, it can seem impossible to reestablish.

Therefore, trust levels remain low, and access to the human potential remains restricted. Failure at co-creation is almost guaranteed when stakeholders believe that trust is earned.

Thankfully, a better approach exists that is more suitable for co-creation. We call it "trust as an investment." When stakeholders view trust as an investment, they can cultivate it consciously and in unlimited quantities if they choose. When co-creation teams embrace this approach, they free themselves from the cognitive bias and emotional constraints of the "trust as earned" approach.

It's commonly accepted that Albert Einstein said, "The most important decision we make is whether we believe we live in a friendly or hostile universe." When co-creation teams resolve to invest trust, they affirm the conviction that the universe is friendly. They do so not because it is safe, secure, or predictable, but because it has endowed them with the inner resources to thrive in a co-creative environment with composure and clarity.

7. **Everyone commits 100 percent.** Full commitment is about removing the option to retreat. We have found that there is usually a difference in what people think they are committing and what they actually commit. Picture a lifeboat. This boat is 100 percent leakproof. It won't sink unless hit by unforeseen external forces—like a tidal wave. The boat and everyone in it will survive. Now imagine that lifeboat has a tiny hole in the hull, below the waterline. Unless the people on the lifeboat have a way to fix the hole, that tiny flaw will eventually sink the boat, and everyone will drown. That's what happens when everyone isn't committed 100 percent. Ninety-nine percent is not enough.

In 334 BCE Alexander the Great, carrying almost 50,000 men in 120 ships, crossed the Dardanelles Strait and landed in the Persian Empire of Darius III. After landing, Alexander ordered his men to burn all the ships. He is believed to have said that "we will either return home in Persian ships or we will die here." Alexander refused to allow retreat to be an option. The lesson here is that your team must have 100 percent commitment to the plan for it to be successful.

Do not keep a back door open. Do not have a Plan B if Plan A fails. The back door allows room for skepticism and only partial commitment from stakeholders. Paul Wagorn, an expert on open innovation, states this nicely: "By removing failure as an option, you are only left with success. Most importantly, you disarm the people who can co-opt your project: the naysayers, the not-invented-here proponents, and the individuals in your organization who may be driven by ego to never be shown up."

Having everyone commit 100 percent means disagreements will occur. This is good! That means everyone is committing. By following the principles we've outlined above, trust will be reinforced and you will continue to progress toward your co-creation goal.

Conclusion

By implementing these principles in your co-creation project, you will ensure everyone commits 100 percent and feels like they belong. Having the right communication also means your stakeholders continually build trust with one another and create value for the project.

Strong leaders facilitate this third Know—the right communication—ensuring that a co-creative team can withstand the inevitable turbulence that will occur from time to time. Remember—cockpits don't have passenger seats. You must either lead the process of communicating the right way or sit in the back and make room for someone else to fly the plane.

CHAPTER 8

The Fourth Know: The Right Execution

We have discussed three of the four Knows: focus, process, and communication. The fourth Know is all about the right execution. It shouldn't be a surprise that the execution of co-creation is where it all comes together. See Figure 8.1 below.

By working with people who have different perspectives and experiences, leaders can create more innovative and effective solutions. However, co-creation can be a challenging experience. For some, it is a radical notion that leaders are no longer the only ones making decisions. Co-creation means realizing that **leadership isn't about managing and controlling—it's about mobilizing and inspiring.** This can be difficult for many people to accept. This process also requires a high degree of trust. Leaders must be willing to give up control and allow their team members to take the reins in many aspects of a project.

Jon Berghoff, the trainer of co-creation consultants we spoke to in Chapter 6, advocates for "a new category of leadership" and believes it is the "calling of our generation."

"It's a shift from an egocentric to an eco-centric way of leading," he said. "It's a shift from knowing to asking. It's a shift from telling to inviting. It's a shift from controlling to unlocking. Where questions are the

Figure 8.1 Co-Creation Model: The Right Execution

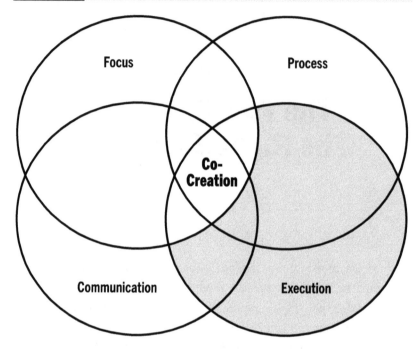

answer. Where the host is the new hero. **Where the sage on the stage is replaced by the guide on the side."**

We couldn't agree more. All the data, concepts, and theories are important—but the execution of these ideas is where the rubber meets the road. And proper execution hinges on the effectiveness of the leader.

Ivan

One of the first courses I had in my doctoral program was on management theory. I vividly remember the professor talking about some obscure concept that baffled me. I raised my hand and asked Dr. Jones (not his real name), "What is the real-world application of this theory?"

He looked at me as though the question annoyed him and said, "Misner, this is a theory class, not an application class. The application of this concept is irrelevant in this course." I was stunned by his answer and raised my hand again. He acknowledged me again, and I exclaimed, "But what good is a theory if you don't know how to apply that concept?"

Dr. Jones, now visibly annoyed, retorted, "Misner, did you not hear me? This is a theory class, not an application class. The execution of this theory is not relevant!" He turned around to write on the chalkboard. I, being fairly young and not very patient with answers that were an "air sandwich," started to raise my hand a third time.

That was when a fellow student (a good 25 years older than me), who also happened to be the deputy director for a major branch of the U.S. government, nudged my arm before I could speak. He looked at me and said, "Shut the [bleep] up, Ivan. This guy is never going to manage anything in his life. Let him drone on with this madness so you can pass the class!" Now that advice had a real-world application, so I shut up.

The deputy director was right. That professor never managed any business, and I, in fact, passed the class and went on to manage a global enterprise. Theory is only as good as its execution, and execution is critical to the implementation of any strategy.

Leaders as Vision Champions

The real-world application of any concept is critical if you want it to truly impact people and the company they work for. It takes a special type of leader to execute on co-creation. Leading a co-creative process must begin by displaying a quiet confidence in everyone else's abilities. **Co-creative leaders are somewhat like conductors of a symphony.** Their role is to unify the performers, set the tempo, and keep the orchestra playing in time and in sync. In effect, they are the vision champions. They maintain the big picture of the overriding objective while allowing everyone to add their unique contributions to the crowdsourced result.

As the world becomes ever more complex and interconnected, the traditional top-down approach to leadership is no longer effective. To create lasting change, leaders must learn to co-create with their teams by identifying team members' strengths, creating a safe environment where everyone feels heard and respected, and leveraging their abilities to achieve collective success.

Leaders can hold the vision in many ways:

- **By clarifying expectations.** Leaders must be clear about what they want to achieve and why it's important. They must also be open to input from all team members. Only then can the team reach consensus and move forward together—and, as always, in alignment with the overarching vision.

- **By leveraging contextual intelligence.** Leaders must be able to adapt their plans and strategies when circumstances change. They must also be able to identify potential saboteurs and manage conflict effectively.

- **By asking questions.** Leaders can derive great value from co-creative teams simply by asking good questions. When do we want to get this done? When do we want to make this decision? What is our ultimate goal for this project? What is stopping us from achieving this success? Routinely asking good questions has the effect of reinforcing consensus and ensuring a cohesive vision among all stakeholders.

- **By leading from behind—and with guardrails.** Sometimes leading a co-creative process can seem like your team is running on a field, and you are running behind them, hollering, just trying to keep them inside the boundaries. In fact, co-creation often means leading from behind. That ensures the leader can keep the big picture—the vision, the boundaries—in mind while everyone is working their way down the field. This approach also positions the leader to gather as much input and extract as much value as possible from each team member.

- **By coaching and cultivating.** Leaders must relinquish control and focus instead on coaching others to perform at their best. By identifying each team member's strengths, the leader can position them to contribute based on their individual talents.

- **By communicating.** As we expressed in Chapter 7, clear and effective communication is necessary among all stakeholders for co-creation projects to succeed. We believe in the communication saturation approach that Richard modeled in our co-creation story.

Positioning the leader as the vision holder in a co-creative process also helps destroy the old model of command and control—of lead, follow, or get out of my way—and help everyone embrace this 3rd Paradigm.

Above all else, the leader must be an example for others to follow. They must be open-minded, respectful, professional, nonjudgmental, humble, transparent, and appreciative. More than that, their actions must embody the project's vision—the mutually desired outcome. Otherwise, they will drag the entire process down. Our open-ended survey responses contained an astounding 1,945 mentions of the word "leader" when discussing the benefits and drawbacks of co-creation. And these responses were NOT to questions about leadership. Strong leaders are crucial to a successful co-creative process.

Barriers to Execution

Even when leaders are committed to holding the vision throughout co-creation, internal barriers can emerge—emotional and psychological ones—that can crop up and cause problems for you. If you are leading a co-creative process, be wary of the following issues:

- **Procrastination.** Co-creation is a dynamic and sometimes messy process. Kicking the can down the road only ensures co-creation won't happen. Don't succumb to the impulse to put things off.

- **Lack of transparency.** Execution of co-creation must be transparent, as we mentioned in Chapter 7. Co-creation will fail if you are not transparent with all stakeholders.

- **Denial and/or avoidance.** Denying there is a problem, miscommunication, or any other issue almost guarantees poor morale. Trying to avoid dealing with a problem only creates more problems.

- **Perfectionism.** LinkedIn co-founder Reid Hoffman has said, "If you're not embarrassed by the first version of your product, you've launched too late." If you demand perfection from your team, the co-creative project will almost certainly fail. Always strive for further improvement, but never let imperfections restrict the co-creative process.

- **Lack of humility.** *Humble people don't think less of themselves, they just think of themselves less.* The lack of humility can be a problem for co-creation because it can lead to individuals prioritizing their own ideas and perspectives over those of others, hindering collaboration and stifling creativity. Additionally, a lack of humility can create a competitive and confrontational atmosphere, which can ultimately impede progress towards the shared goal.

Leaders must not only hold the vision of the co-creative project, but they must also hold themselves accountable. Recognizing and dealing with these barriers is a good place to start.

Decision Making

Even in co-creative processes, someone must have ultimate decision-making authority. Consider the following three approaches to decision making as you form and guide your co-creative team. You can see how they correlate to each of the paradigms (see Figure 8.2 below):

1. **Authority.** *If you want to run a co-creative process, exercise authoritative decision making about as often as you see a solar eclipse.* With authoritative decision making, team members have a high level of direction, but the risk of someone throwing a grenade during the process increases exponentially over a team making decisions by consensus. Authoritative decision making is closely aligned with the 1st Paradigm and can substantially reduce the morale of a group using the Co-Creation Model.

2. **Majority.** Decision making through majority opinion can result in some disengagement because some people always lose. Dissatisfied team members might try to undermine the

Figure 8.2 Decision Making and the Three Paradigms

co-creative process. You must use this sparingly if you want to keep all members engaged. Decision through majority opinion often occurs in the 2nd Paradigm—people are collaborative but there are still winners and losers.

3. **Consensus.** Decision making through consensus is typically the slowest approach, but it results in high collaboration and a feeling that everyone wins. This is the type of decision making we recommend for co-creative projects and organizations. To help speed things along, structure the decision-making process so that the team achieves consensus in a set amount of time (whether that's one meeting or six months). Once the time is up, you can guide the team toward a general consensus, where everyone agrees to move forward on a chosen path, even if they are not in 100 percent agreement.

Survey Analysis by Age and Gender

Feedback from people who have participated in co-creation is invaluable. Their collective input is a playbook for the leader of the team. As mentioned earlier, we surveyed more than 4,200 individuals for this book about the dos and don'ts of co-creation. When it comes to the respondents' age and their belief in co-creation as a viable strategy, there is a significant shift against it among people who are 60 and older. Although the vast majority of people we surveyed believed in the value of co-creation, those who did not believe in it were likely to be older. Less than 10 percent of people who did not believe in its value were 39 or younger. Knowing this data point is important when working with more mature team members. There may be more resistance to co-creation in this more seasoned demographic. In fact, one of our survey respondents over 60 years of age came right out and stated that co-creation *"is a bunch of happy-talking nonsense."* While we chuckled as we read his response (yes, it was a man), it did clearly show us that the concept is not universally accepted, and it supported the finding that there could be a stronger resistance to it from older professionals. See Figure 8.3 below.

People younger than 40 were much more receptive to the co-creative process than people 60 or older. The trend line supporting a co-creative process continues to increase for older groups up to 59 years of age, until it drops off dramatically at 60 years and above.

What this means for anyone implementing a co-creative process within their organization is that their more mature workers may not be nearly as receptive to this type of interaction as those who are younger. Clearly this will not apply to each individual employee, but you should take it into account when attempting to implement the Four Knows in your business.

Figure 8.3 Co-creation by Age

Age	39 and under	40 – 49	50 – 59	60 and over
Co-creation: Yes	24.20%	27.73%	29.43%	18.64%
Co-creation: No	9.68%	29.03%	29.03%	32.26%

Regarding gender, we found that overall, both men and women felt that co-creation was a valuable process in an organization. However, people who did *not* feel that it was a viable strategy were more likely to be men than women. More than half, 58 percent, of the people who were not supportive of a co-creative process were men, and just under 43 percent were women.

Execution and the Top Benefits of Co-Creation

Below we've expanded on our earlier discussion of the benefits of co-creation, as identified by our survey respondents, so you are more equipped to leverage these perceived benefits when executing co-creation. We've analyzed, synthesized, and interpreted the data so leaders can take action based on each of these insights.

Benefit 1: Diversity of Ideas

The diversity of ideas and perspectives is essential for successful co-creation. Even if people are not experts in a particular field, they can still contribute valuable insights. The best project results come from working across cultures and with many different positions. This allows for a broader range of input and helps fill skill gaps. Age, ethnicity, interests, and connections all play a role and should be considered when forming a co-creation team. A key factor to obtaining substantial diversity of ideas within a group is to focus on inclusion. Diversity is a fact—a group either has it or they do not have it. Inclusion is a choice. It is a choice that when done well, leads to diversity relating to the makeup of the group and subsequently to the diversity of ideas presented by the group.

To execute on co-creation, everyone on the team should be trained that the "diversity of ideas" is a strength. It may often be frustrating as well, but it is definitely a strength. One survey respondent lamented that the technical people on a project they were involved in "were too focused on the technical issues relating to the process." Another individual complained that "the marketing people were too focused on the marketing aspects of the project." **It is the diversity of ideas that makes co-creation work, because often individual team members are too focused on their limited perspectives.** So if the leaders persuasively explain why diverse ideas are critical to the process, execution will be more effective in

It is the diversity of ideas that makes co-creation work, because often individual team members are too focused on their limited perspectives.

this area. People don't care about how to do something until they understand why they need to do something. Communicating the power of different perspectives is a crucial task for co-creative leaders.

Steps to take:

- Be inclusive in the makeup of co-creative teams. Include subject matter experts, specialists, big vision thinkers, true believers, and skeptics. Put a barking dog in the group—a person who speaks up at every point of contention—to ensure people offer their concerns in front of you and not behind your back.

- Make room for people to share their ideas in a variety of ways, including through dialogue and writing.

- Make sure everyone speaks. Go around the room and ask all team members for their ideas. If someone has nothing to share, say, "I'll come back to you"—and then remember to circle back to them later.

Benefit 2: Learning from Each Other

The power of brainstorming comes from the fresh ideas and new perspectives that emerge when people come together. As a team, people can learn from each other and create a better product or service as a result. **All of us are better than one of us.**

One survey respondent wrote, "Sometimes people think they know the solution when they don't fully understand the problem." They added that through the open dialogue that was encouraged during a project, people realized that the solution they had didn't actually address the problem. "One person in particular did a 180-degree turn when they saw the full picture from several other people's perspective."

In organizations with more than 100 employees (as seen in Figure 8.4 below), "learning from each other" rated significantly higher than any of the other benefits of co-creation. Based on various comments from survey respondents, that is most likely because employees in larger organizations don't understand the complexity of various departments, as well as employees would at smaller companies.

Larger organizations tend to be more "silo oriented" because they often have more layers of management and a more complex organizational

Figure 8.4 Number of People in an Organization by Top 7 Benefits

Number of people in organization	10 or fewer	11 – 100	Over 100
Diversity of ideas	69.57%	67.59%	69.80%
Learning from each other	60.81%	62.26%	68.60%
Stronger relationships	48.42%	52.51%	52.0%
Seeing areas of the business that you don't see	50.29%	47.59%	45.0%
More empowered team/shared feeling of ownership	46.70%	47.28%	48.80%
Increased quality of creativity	46.70%	48.31%	44.80%
Shared resources	45.42%	47.69%	44.80%

structure, which can lead to departments becoming more isolated from each other. In addition, communication channels can become more formalized and bureaucratic, making it difficult for employees to collaborate across departments. Smaller organizations, on the other hand, tend to have a flatter organizational structure and fewer layers of management, which can facilitate more open communication and collaboration between departments.

Steps to take:

- Shut up! You might be the leader, but you shouldn't monopolize the meetings.
- Although you want a barking dog in the group, don't let them take over the meetings. You don't want anyone to feel like they have to yell just to be heard.
- Reiterate to all stakeholders the important principle of "listen to learn" (see below) as one survey respondent called it.
- Implement mechanisms to ensure people don't get interrupted. Two great examples are a talking stick, where only the person holding the stick can talk, or a time limit for the speaker. For the latter, if the person speaking goes over their allotted time but everyone wants them to keep going, the group as a whole can say, "Continue; tell us more."
- Ensure people learn from each other by ending meetings with questions like "What did we learn today that we didn't know? What did you learn today that you didn't know before?"

- Consider asking everyone at every meeting to write down something they learned from someone in a completely different area. This is a great technique for anchoring the new learning because writing down new information you hear helps you remember it better. This also creates a log of all the new things people learned.

"Listen to learn" is a concept that emphasizes the importance of actively listening in order to acquire knowledge and understanding. It involves actively paying attention to what someone else is saying, processing their words and ideas, and using that information to increase your own knowledge and understanding.

Listening to learn can be applied in a variety of contexts, such as in academic settings, workplace environments, personal relationships, and everyday interactions. In each of these contexts, listening to learn involves setting aside preconceptions and biases, asking questions to clarify understanding, and being open to new perspectives and ideas.

Effective listening to learn involves several key skills, including being present in the moment, maintaining focus on the speaker, practicing empathy, and engaging in active listening techniques such as paraphrasing, summarizing, and reflecting back what you have heard.

By adopting a "listen to learn" approach, individuals can enhance their ability to learn from others, deepen their understanding of complex concepts and issues, and build stronger connections with others.

Benefit 3: Stronger Relationships

When people work together in teams, relationships are created and strengthened. They can lead to the development of synergies, which can have a positive impact on performance.

Engagement is key to developing strong relationships. When people are involved and feel like they have a say in the process, it leads to buy-in and trust. This can result in long-term relationships that enhance the performance of multiple departments.

When people know that the co-creative process isn't a top-down approach, it leads to a powerful, positive culture shift and growth for all involved! One survey participant shared, "Involving others in our organization has led to stronger relationships and improved performance."

The shared consciousness of a group of people can be a resource of their collective wisdom when handled correctly. But things can go off the rails if people start getting overly aggressive in the discussions. As one person in the survey pointed out, **"You can disagree without being disagreeable."** As a leader, repeat this mantra regularly to participants in a co-creative process.

Steps to take:

- Guide the team to avoid being "clumpy." People naturally "clump" together with other people they know or who are similar to them. Encourage team members to go to lunch or have coffee with someone in another department. Suggest they meet informally outside designated co-creative meeting times. By getting to know team members outside their comfort zones, stakeholders will build stronger relationships.

- Remind team members that a strong relationship doesn't happen by chance. This is advice they can carry with them long after a co-creative project is finished. As the leader, establish dedicated social times to build relationships.

- Promote virtual meetings to strengthen remote teams. Technology flattens the communication hierarchy and enables people to build relationships without ever having met in person.

Benefit 4: Seeing Areas of the Business That You Don't See

Working with a team of experts from different disciplines can help you come across unseen areas of the business and discover new solutions.

Each team member brings their own unique perspective to the table, which can help uncover issues that you wouldn't otherwise perceive or understand. By looking at things from different angles, you can gain a more comprehensive view of the problem and find more innovative solutions.

Examining things from other people's perspectives can be incredibly insightful and helpful in finding new solutions to problems. It's important to make use of this resource to create the most efficient and innovative solutions possible.

One survey respondent said, "The process of co-creation gave a more complete vision of the entire organization to all the people working on the project. This in turn enabled everyone to see areas of the business that they were unaware of." Having this kind of perspective is extremely helpful.

Steps to take:

- Point out the things you didn't realize as the leader and highlight what you see now—new elements of the business—during the co-creative process.

- Get other team members to share what they see now that they didn't notice before; this dusts off the gray matter and keeps people engaged.

- Realize that this won't work if the team isn't diverse. Seek out different perspectives. **Your team will be unstoppable if everyone can get past the discomfort of hearing information they personally might not be interested in but is important to the project as a whole.**

- Ask team members good questions: What do you see in this that affects your department/office/region specifically? What excites you about this project? What are you most proud of at this point in the project?

Benefit 5: More Empowered Teams/Shared Sense of Ownership

When teams are empowered and have a shared sense of ownership, they are more likely to succeed. Empowered teams have a vested interest in the outcome and are more likely to put forth the best effort. Creating team alignment gives everyone that sense of shared ownership for the project.

The team system is slower than the approach the clients are used to, but it creates better services for them because all team members are working toward a common goal. Getting the sales team, production team, and administrative team working together creates a stronger organizational team. One survey respondent said, "In the co-creative process, you give up control but you gain engagement from a broader number of organizational stakeholders."

Our survey results showed that there is a statistically significant difference between men and women in regard to "more empowered teams and a stronger sense of ownership." As you can see below, a significantly higher percentage of women feel this is an important factor in the process of co-creation.

We asked a colleague of ours, Sam Horn, author of *Tongue Fu!*, how she interpreted this data. She said she felt that "women truly value an empowered team and sense of ownership because for so long our voice was not always welcome in a company setting. In the early days of my career, women were often 'talked over.' The process of open discussion and full engagement gives women a more equal opportunity to contribute our experience and expertise, and that's a win for everyone."

As you can see in Figure 8.5 below, this interpretation appears to have great validity. There is a 10 percent difference between men and women's attitudes toward this benefit of co-creation. It is the largest difference between the genders when it comes to the benefits of the process.

Steps to take:

- Send a survey or email to all team members and request that everyone responds. This is critical to ensure everyone feels they are being heard. Ask questions like the following:
  - ▶ How happy are you with the way the project is going?
  - ▶ Do you feel like you're being heard?
  - ▶ Have you been able to contribute your ideas?
  - ▶ Do you feel like other people's input is valuable?
  - ▶ What would you do differently to move this project forward?
  - ▶ Do you feel you're being held back in any way?
- Set expectations for your team at the outset that while all ideas are valued, not all can be accepted. This way, people will retain a sense of ownership over the project even if their idea is not implemented. If you fail to set these expectations, people will default to

Figure 8.5 Gender by Top 7 Benefits

Gender	Male	Female
Diversity of ideas	67.42%	71.07%
Learning from each other	60.30%	64.06%
Stronger relationships	47.32%	52.57%
Seeing areas of the business that you don't see	47.99%	50.20%
More empowered team/shared feeling of ownership	42.41%	52.32%
Increased quality of creativity	46.37%	47.38%
Shared resources	42.72%	49.40%

believing, "I gave them ideas and they didn't listen to anything I said." To foster ongoing ownership, say something like "If any of you feel your ideas aren't being heard, see me after the meeting."

- Be persistent in your efforts to build and maintain a shared sense of ownership. The suggestions above are not "one and done;" ownership is something leaders should constantly work on. Periodically check in with everyone and ask questions like the following:
  - ► How are we doing on our vision?
  - ► Are we getting there?
  - ► Are we going in the right direction? In the wrong direction?

Benefit 6: Increased Quality of Creativity

In today's business world, you must think creatively to stay ahead of the competition. When different people with diverse backgrounds and perspectives come together, they can generate new and innovative ideas. This creativity can lead to higher-quality results and help take your organization to the next level.

Creativity is the result of thinking and talking together. Brainstorming sessions can be crucial because they allow everyone to talk through their ideas and work on the problem at a deeper level. These sessions require a complete focus on the problem at hand and a shared commitment to contemplating the myriad of potential solutions available.

Ivan

I remember a time early in my career when I was a management consultant, leading a team to develop a strategic plan. Stakeholders told me what they had in mind, but I could sense their ideas were shallow—stemming from individual gut responses to my questions rather than the deep thought that occurs when people channel their energy and brainstorm a problem together.

Once I presented their ideas back to them, they quickly realized their plan wasn't on target. They had yet to harness their collective brainpower to find a solution. But this exercise had made the team realize it's easier to write a plan than execute a plan. They hadn't yet put time and effort into the task and thought about the speed bumps, problems, and unintended consequences of their decisions. There really is no way to get around this step. But once they put their heads together and devoted the necessary brainpower to it, they became more creative and developed a much more compelling strategic plan.

Steps to take:

- Encourage creativity by relentlessly asking questions. Tell people to think about their ideas and get back to the group. Creativity must be nurtured.

- Create space for all ideas: the good, the bad, and the ugly. Set expectations that no idea should be disregarded immediately. **Hold yourself accountable and do not shoot down ideas.** The following survey response is telling in this regard: "A VP asked for 'open sky brainstorming' and said 'everything is on the table' in an effort to help create innovation in a very competitive market. The first suggestion made was shot down immediately with an 'except that' attitude. Four of the ten people in the room walked out…the negatives this created set us back rather than helped us advance…ego got in the way."

- Creativity is usually an expression of compassion; it comes from the sincere desire to make someone's life better or alleviate someone's pain. As a leader, strive to get your team to care about your customers or some other stakeholder—if you succeed, you'll be amazed at the creative solutions people suggest.

Benefit 7: Shared Resources

Sharing resources with others can be extremely valuable. By pooling skills and talents, you can free up time for other activities and build stronger relationships between individuals and groups. It also allows people to see aspects of the operation, from design to execution, in new ways.

Bringing additional resources to a project also increases the client's confidence. When people have more information, they make better decisions. People with different perspectives on a problem can offer better solutions. Thus, sharing resources is an important way to improve efficiency and results.

In our survey, the benefit of "sharing resources" showed the second largest difference between men and women. Women found this benefit of co-creation more important than men did by a statistically significant margin. Younger respondents (particularly those under 30) also felt that it was a substantial benefit compared to older respondents. See Figure 8.6 below.

Steps to take:

- Pool your resources to achieve the mutually desired outcome. Shared resources can flip the perception that your challenges exceed your resources, which is often a major frustration for individuals and organizations.

- Lead by example: Team member often believe the leader has access to more resources. Demonstrate your willingness to be generous with resources.

- Go around the room and ask every person, "What do you need?" Make sure you get a response from all of them. When you are aware of their need, resources are a way to respond to that, and your team will likely be surprised by how well they can support each other.

- Facilitate connections. Create connections and develop team members so they can learn to do it as well.

Figure 8.6 Age by Top 7 Benefits

Age	29 or under	30 – 39	40 – 49	50 – 59	60 or over
Diversity of ideas	73.46%	67.83%	67.58%	68.88%	72.05%
Learning from each other	67.77%	63.59%	63.72%	59.58%	60.48%
Stronger relationships	45.50%	49.0%	46.74%	51.90%	52.99%
Seeing areas of the business that you don't see	47.87%	50.75%	46.74%	49.56%	50.19%
More empowered team/shared feeling of ownership	37.91%	42.14%	44.60%	51.58%	51.21%
Increased quality of creativity	54.03%	47.13%	46.83%	44.62%	48.16%
Shared resources	56.87%	46.38%	46.31%	43.90%	44.85%

- Remember that identifying needs is the doorway to resources. Have a conversation with your stakeholders dedicated to needs. What do we need to achieve our mutually desired outcome? What do we need to communicate effectively? What does the co-creative framework need? What does the project need to ensure its success? These are all straightforward questions; there's no reason to be clever when trying to identify needs.

For a co-creative process to succeed, the leader should focus on solutions. The seven top benefits of co-creation we have focused on throughout the book not only demonstrate the advantages of co-creation but also provide the solutions to address challenges that emerge. By focusing on these positive aspects of co-creation, leaders can maximize the benefits.

Co-Creation Drawbacks Leaders Must Consider

Just as we analyzed, synthesized, and interpreted the survey results for the top seven benefits of co-creation, we also did so for the top seven drawbacks, as we discussed in Chapter 3. Leaders should keep in mind the following so they are aware of these drawbacks and can neutralize them.

Note: Some of this information might feel repetitive, but as we are drawing close to the end of the book, we feel we should highlight these findings from the perspective of execution, so you can avoid these pitfalls.

Drawback 1: Personality Conflicts

Personality conflicts can often derail the co-creative process. Arguments and disagreements can slow down or even stop the progress of a project. If left unchecked, these conflicts can become toxic and undermine the entire project. It is important to have a leader in place who can identify and remove people who are causing problems.

One person may try to control the direction of the project, while others may not get along due to different temperaments. This can create chaos and make it difficult to move forward. In some cases, people may deliberately undermine the project in order to cause problems for any number of reasons such as protecting their turf, trying to undermine someone else, or to control the direction of the project.

It's important to be able to discuss opposing opinions openly and respectfully. But if different temperaments clash, the loudest person may try to come out on top, leading to competitiveness and chaos within the team. By remaining open-minded and respectful of others' opinions, you can resolve personality conflicts and move forward with the co-creative process.

Moreover, by remaining calm and constructive, you can help keep the peace on your team and maintain a positive, productive work environment.

Steps to take:

- Set expectations. Laying the ground rules down with people of what is acceptable behavior and what is unacceptable. Even in a process filled with disagreement, as co-creation often is, all stakeholders must remain professional.

- Proactively establish a response plan for when disagreements arise. We recommend a "disagree and commit" approach, where you create a plan for dealing with disagreements in advance. That way, co-creative teams know the process for handling disagreements and can act even if they are in conflict. For instance, your team might vote to settle disagreements.

- Remind the team or people in conflict of the team or organization's underlying core values, and how they relate to the mutually desired outcome. **Core values establish boundaries for expectations of professional behavior.**

- Respond quickly when you see people behaving badly. Praise them in public and redirect them in private.

- People have two ears and one mouth, so remind team members to use them proportionally. If needed, use techniques like the talking stick (discussed earlier in this chapter) to regulate speaking time.

- Eject anyone who uses physical violence. Physical confrontation is a nonstarter.

- Consider the overall framework for engagement and decision making.

Drawback 2: Dealing with Egos

One of the most challenging aspects of working in a co-creative environment is dealing with egos. More than half of all survey respondents across all age groups viewed dealing with egos as a drawback. Notably, more than 60 percent of people 50 and older shared this concern. For respondents over 60, dealing with egos surfaced as their top concern (63.96 percent), with the related issue of personality conflicts following close behind (58.12 percent). For this group, these two concerns greatly outpaced the other top drawbacks, which ranged from 35.91 percent to 37.06 percent.

Egos can lead to power struggles and undermine healthy collaboration. A complicating factor is that **toxic people with strong egos often don't know they are toxic! They are clueless to the fact that they are creating chaos and tend to blame other people for the problem.**

Egos can be tamed by cultivating a "we vs. me" mentality, in which team members focus less on themselves, are more open to feedback, and take joy in the success of others. See Figure 8.7 below.

Steps to take:

- Acknowledge the ego. Sometimes the best way to deal with an outsize ego is simply to acknowledge it. This can help defuse any tension that may be brewing.

- Avoid power struggles. If egos are leading to power struggles, it's important to try to redirect the attention of the parties involved by having them focus on the mutually desired outcome—reminding them of the shared mission, vision, goals, and tactics.

- Before meetings, set a time limit for how long people can speak—and assign a timekeeper. As previously mentioned, you can also use a physical object during meetings to limit overtalking and interruptions by only allowing the person holding the object to speak.

- When conflicts arise and people disagree, use "The Elusive And" strategy from the book Crucial Conversations (by Kerry Patterson et al., 2002). Ask, "Is there a way to do X while accomplishing Y?"

- Focus on the action, not the person. If you need to talk about someone's problematic behavior, focus on what they did, rather than on them, so they won't feel attacked.

Drawback 3: Poor Communication

One of the most common issues that people have in interactions with others is communication. Often, people feel they are not being heard or that their input is not valued. This can be especially frustrating when it comes to projects you are passionate about.

One way to combat this issue is to ensure that there is open communication throughout the entire process, which we detailed in Chapter 7.

Figure 8.7 Age by Top 7 Drawbacks

Age	29 or under	30 – 39	40 – 49	50 – 59	60 or over
Personality conflicts	58.29%	54.86%	57.80%	60.95%	58.12%
Dealing with egos	51.18%	53.12%	53.86%	60.15%	63.96%
Poor communication	55.92%	49.0%	39.54%	40.10%	37.06%
People who don't pull their weight	45.97%	38.90%	39.97%	38.80%	39.59%
Lack of agreement on who makes the final decision	36.97%	38.53%	34.99%	37.67%	37.18%
Individuals hijacking the project direction	25.59%	30.80%	36.62%	38.40%	39.09%
Non-aligned vision for the project	33.65%	31.17%	31.39%	35.25%	35.91%

This means being transparent about what is happening and where the project stands. It also means having regular dialogue with all participants so that everyone understands what is going on.

If you can saturate your environment with communication, it will go a long way toward ensuring successful human interaction, as will being transparent in your leadership and communication.

The crosstabulation in Figure 8.7 above most notably shows a disparity between professionals younger than 30 and those 30 and older when it comes to perceiving a problem with poor communication. Nearly 56 percent of professionals younger than 30 identified poor communication as a drawback to co-creation. Meanwhile, on average, slightly less than 40 percent of professionals older than 30 held the same viewpoint. The fact that communication was a bigger concern for younger stakeholders is a factor that should be taken into consideration while working through the co-creative process.

Steps to take:

- Be an active listener (and coach your team to be the same). During conversations and meetings, ask yourself four questions: What was said? What did I hear? What did it mean? How did it change me? If someone is speaking, you should confirm whether you heard the words properly and understood the speaker's meaning correctly. From there, ask yourself how this new knowledge will change your behavior and actions moving forward. If communication doesn't lead to change, or a better understanding of the situation, it's useless.

- Use the communication saturation technique. Provide more information than you think is necessary and only reduce the volume of information as people start exhibiting signs that they have enough. This might play out in people not showing up on video conference calls or not reading various communications.

- Send a communications survey to team members asking a variety of questions: How are we doing on communication? Are you getting enough information? Do you feel like you know what's going on? Adjust your communications strategy in response to the survey results.

- Make sure everyone feels they are getting enough information, especially those who have a history of feeling uninformed (such as people under 30).

Drawback 4: People Who Don't Pull Their Weight

It's frustrating when people don't do their share. Whether it's at work, in a relationship, or in a family, it creates an imbalance that can be difficult to overcome.

When someone shirks their responsibilities, it puts a strain on those forced to pick up the slack. This is especially true if the person who is not carrying their weight is older or of a different gender.

It's important to have a frank discussion with anyone who isn't meeting your expectations. If they're not willing to step up and do their part, you may need to reevaluate your relationship with them. As Richard said in his story (in Chapter 6), **some people are happy in their hole. As the leader of a co-creative project, grab a ladder and start climbing.**

Figure 8.8 below identifies statistically significant differences between the views of men and women in terms of drawbacks to co-creation. People who don't pull their weight are the fourth drawback. Notably, nearly 8 percent more women view this as a drawback than men, making this the greatest difference between women and men in terms of their perception of drawbacks to co-creation. Keep this in mind as you lead co-creative teams—men should be particularly mindful of whether your team members are discontented over the equitable division of labor.

Steps to take:

- Speak privately and directly to the person who is not pulling their weight to discuss the issue and determine how to resolve it. Do not create needless policies, procedures, or protocols for the entire group just to try to correct the behavior of one individual; doing so risks alienating everyone else.
- Be mindful that more women than men recognize people not pulling their weight as a drawback to co-creation. Consider consulting with each team member one-on-one to assess how they feel or periodically conduct an anonymous survey on this topic.

Figure 8.8	Gender by Top 7 Drawbacks		
Gender	Male	Female	Average
Personality conflicts	57.30%	59.32%	58%
Dealing with egos	59.32%	55.09%	57%
Poor communication	38.65%	42.99%	41%
People who don't pull their weight	35.90%	43.85%	40%
Lack of agreement on who makes the final decision	36.17%	37.85%	37%
Individuals hijacking the project direction	37.39%	34.32%	36%
Non-aligned vision of the project	31.80%	35.28%	33%

Make adjustments as necessary based on your conversations and/
or survey results.

Drawback 5: Lack of Agreement on Who Makes the Final Decision

If there is no leader, or if too many people are trying to be the leader, it
can be difficult to reach consensus. This can lead to conflict and a poor
group dynamic. Power fills a vacuum, so when there is no leader, a few
people can move to dominate the group.

Strong leaders who do not rely on "command and control" are crucial
to each incremental step of the co-creative process. It is important that
everyone knows that as key milestones are achieved, there is a leader
who can tie up the process in a collaborative manner. This will help
avoid conflict and ensure that decisions are made efficiently. The leader
must be able to handle the different personalities in the room to allow
everyone to give maximum effort; having a strong leader ensures everyone will be included and eliminates the risk of hijacking by individuals
who are naysayers or out for their own benefit.

Steps to take:

- If it was not determined at the beginning of the co-creation project, identify who is ultimately accountable for decisions and the
  results of the co-creative process. Remember that it takes skillful

leadership to take good ideas and fashion them into positive attributes of the project, and to make people feel included and content with the final output. Strong leadership and communication are vital. Choose a leader (or leaders) wisely.

- Convene the group and speak earnestly if the group dynamics are poor. Speak openly if there is a lack of strong leadership, and work together to address the issue by selecting a leader for the entire co-creative process, or assigning people to lead different parts of the process.

Drawback 6: Individuals Hijacking the Direction of the Project

Some people can have ulterior motives and hijack the direction of the project for their own benefit. This can cause repeated interference outside their area of expertise and lead to a lot of wasted time and effort. One of our survey respondents shared, "We did not have a strong leader. Therefore, the loudest opinionated person spent their time trying to hijack the group discussion, and if it was not their idea, it was a 'rubbish' idea, which demoralized the group, ruining the group's integrity."

Hijacking the direction of a project is extremely frustrating and counterproductive for the rest of the group, and it undermines the trust and cooperation that is necessary for a successful project. Co-creative teams must be able to trust one another to work effectively, and this behavior makes that impossible.

Steps to take:

- As a leader, intervene quickly if you notice someone hijacking the project, to stop them from negatively impacting the project as a whole.
- Speak one-on-one with the hijacker and remind them that while all perspectives are important, trying to redirect the project to suit their goals violates the co-creation approach of having a shared focus and mutually desired outcome.

- Ask them to identify their root concern—perhaps the group can learn from it and address it while still working toward the mutually desired outcome (See Benefit 6: Increased Quality of Creativity on page 142.)

Drawback 7: Nonaligned Vision for the Project

If you don't have a clear, commonly agreed-upon objective for your project, it's easy for discussions to start going in circles. Endless discussion and disagreement can be frustrating, especially if there is no clear end goal in sight.

Make sure that everyone involved in the project understands and agrees with the vision. Once you have buy-in from all sides, you can move forward with confidence, knowing that everyone is working toward the same goal. Without a shared vision, it's all too easy for projects to get derailed.

This is where company culture plays a critical role. **Culture eats strategy for breakfast. It is the secret sauce to a successful organization and can be effectively used in a healthy co-creative process.** A strong company culture can enable co-creative teams to overcome even the most challenging obstacles.

Culture eats strategy for breakfast. It is the secret sauce to a successful organization and can be effectively used in a healthy co-creative process.

Steps to take:

- Stay positive and remain committed to the goal, even when things get tough.
- Remember to focus on the vision, not the obstacles. When challenges arise, remind everyone that together the team will achieve great things if they stay committed to the vision.
- If the overarching company or team culture is lacking, implement team-building activities to help strengthen it.

By being aware of these seven drawbacks, strong leaders can manage more effectively throughout the co-creative process.

THE STORY

The story resumes with Richard really stepping into his role of co-creation leader—managing both the advantages and drawbacks of the 3rd Paradigm.

Richard understood the challenges he was facing, but he also knew the potential power of co-creation and crowdsourcing. He had read *The Wisdom of Crowds* by James Surowiecki and understood that when a crowd is suitably motivated, sufficiently diverse, and independent, it is far more intelligent than any individual could ever be. The key was to channel that motivation and diversity into a functional platform that would work for everyone.

He knew that the shared consciousness of the people in his organization was a depository of their collective wisdom. He remembered the example in *Wisdom of Crowds* about the TV game show *Who Wants to be a Millionaire.* The "Ask the Audience" lifeline, where the contestant could use the audience to help them answer the question, had the correct answer 91 percent of the time, which was substantially higher than any other lifeline in the show. He now planned to harness the collective intelligence of his organization to get this project to completion.

Richard gave great consideration to what his role would be in completing the platform. **He understood that he was not only the conductor of this symphony. He was the champion of his vision.** It was his primary task to hold the vision and continuously convey it to all the parties who were co-creating the platform—the result of that vision. Now the hard work of implementation had to begin.

Richard's number-one concern was the potential for personality conflicts. He witnessed that challenge early in the co-creative process, when one of his tech people said that "he felt like he was swimming in a pool with sharks" when he was talking to franchisees. Their force of personality was overwhelming, and it made him feel he couldn't do his work effectively. Another person on the project said that the animus that occurred when a team member didn't respect another member's experience and knowledge halted the work that was being done. The inevitable personality conflicts needed to be dealt with by skilled project leaders. Therefore, **finding the right leaders to manage the co-creative process—and the strong personalities involved—was of paramount importance.**

On the other hand, he also knew that the diversity of ideas was the biggest strength of the co-creative approach, so many different personalities were inevitable. It was important to build in feedback mechanisms that allowed people to interact and give each other suggestions and observations in a productive manner.

The process of co-creation began by triaging the list of issues they had created at the preconference meeting. From that list, they created a matrix, which they then compared against the company's main key performance indicators (KPIs). The items that matched all or most of the KPIs took the highest priority. This matrix was an objective measure, and that helped manage the personality clashes. One person on the project noted that some of those whose ideas weren't at the top of the list still got upset, so **the process would occasionally blow up, but with good leadership it coalesced into an operational plan.**

A related problem with personality conflicts was the issue of egos. Richard understood that the co-creative process required him to continually remind people of the big picture and nudge them to do the "right thing" for the project, not just the right thing for them. It was absolutely key for people to **think of the vision, not the obstacles.** When team members did that, they could release their ego-driven agenda and look toward the overall goal of the project.

It turned out to be a learning experience for everyone. By working with individuals in other departments and other parts of the world, they learned about many new facets of the business (both good and bad). It was an opportunity to speak to people in other countries and not remain isolated in their own corner of the world.

However, it was important to be prepared for the fact that they would not always agree with one another. In fact, discussions could get fairly heated, especially when a little vested self-interest seemed to be at play.

Richard heard about one session headed by a very strong leader of co-creation in the company, in which there was a lot of disagreement over a specific issue. A heated debate ensued, and one of the participants leaned over to the person running the meeting and told him he should step in. The leader calmly whispered back, "I want to let everyone hash it out so they understand the complexity of the issue and can see the various sides of it. They have much to learn from one another, but they can never get there if they don't talk it out. It usually works out when people come to a conclusion because they talked it through." Interestingly, that is exactly what happened. He acted as a guardrail to keep things from getting too hot but allowed the participants to actively disagree with one another, and that process led to a fully co-created decision.

Conclusion

We wanted to close this chapter on execution and leadership by amplifying the voices of our survey participants. Let the leader in you hear what they are saying:

"Good leadership was able to bring out the best in people and gave an open/free atmosphere of sharing ideas, resulting in a successful outcome."

"I worked with a number of people over the years. One group stands out because the six people involved respected each other and were able to listen and contribute to the projects, whether they were construction projects or developing new services to implement. Ideas are important, no matter where they come from. The key is to have a leader who can define or visualize the goal of the project."

"We created a baseline way of communication through a mastermind group. Then the nine participants met for a two-day ideation process. We created 67 ideas and decided to execute on two of them to move forward with and bring to market. We estimate these products will account for a 20 percent revenue growth in the first year and up to 35 percent growth in the second year of implementation. In addition, we created a culture of open communication and zero blame while creating leaders in the organization."

"Some people are great at one thing, and some are great at others. When good people can get on the same page, great things can happen. Ego is the main killer for any team effort."

"Brainstorming ideas always leads to innovative new solutions that a single person may overlook…and two (or more) heads are always better than one."

"Without clear leadership, a group project is only as good as the leader."

"I have found that older members of leadership are resistant to accepting input from underlings, and if they are over the other members of the team in the management hierarchy, then they sometimes shut down new ideas because they don't understand them."

"Good leadership was able to bring out the best in people and gave an open/free atmosphere of sharing ideas, resulting in a successful outcome."

"There needs to be a clear vision on the outset regarding the goals and the steps to achieve those goals. Each person has to have ownership. There needs to be a leader, but each person on the team must have a clear understanding of their responsibility and role. The old hierarchy of one leader at the top doesn't work anymore!!!"

CHAPTER 9

Achieving Success with the Co-Creation Model

This short chapter summarizes some of the content we shared and completes the story before we move to the final chapter, an interview with the three authors.

The Co-Creation Model can guide implementation of co-creation in your own organization, but it is not always easy. Even still, the rewards are worth the effort. Co-creation can lead to explosive revenue growth, increased profitability, and truly inclusive work cultures.

The Four Knows described in the previous chapters provide a model for you to follow—a model that can help you mitigate the challenges that our story's protagonist, Richard, encountered. With our first Know, **Focus,** a co-creative team must establish a mutually desired outcome. The second Know, **Process,** requires the team to create an underlying framework to guide their co-creation. The third Know, **Communication,** underscores the critical importance of open, clear communication among all stakeholders. The fourth Know, **Execution,** requires good leadership to guide the co-creative team to a successful outcome. The point at which each of these Knows overlap is where we achieve true co-creation. See Figure 9.1 below.

Our research and personal experiences have highlighted the many benefits and challenges of co-creation throughout this book—just as

Figure 9.1 Co-Creation Model: The Intersection of All Four Knows

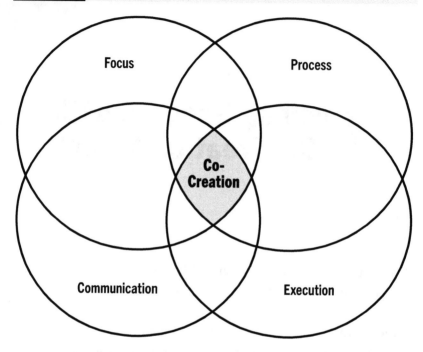

Richard's story has revealed. We leave you with the conclusion of that story—how Richard dealt with problems, persevered, and guided his company to a new level of success.

THE STORY

We pick up Richard's story with him guiding (but not dictating) the co-creative process. Always holding the vision, Richard led his stakeholders through the lengthy process of launching a new plat-form that met the needs of their growing organization.

In a private discussion with one of his associates after a frustrating encounter dealing with all the opinions being shared during the co-creative process, Richard groaned, **"I've created my own co-creation hell!"** His associate said, "No, no, we need more people engaged in the process; this is really hard, but we are getting great results!" He pointed out that the more people they got on board, the more buy-in they would have. "We are developing this project into a team of co-creators," he added. "That's what is making this work." Richard reminded himself that co-creation is a thing of beauty and a muddy mess. It can be both at the same time.

One thing was certain: Most people working on the project had clearly developed a sense of ownership, and they were more empowered than they had been before. And no matter how tiring it was to herd cats while holding the vision, things were progressing incredibly well—much better than they had under the previous two paradigms.

Richard also had to remain vigilant about **individuals hijacking the direction of the project.** It was easy to go down rabbit holes that someone had a lot of energy on. Sometimes there was a fine line between having people feel empowered and having them try to take over some element of the effort. He had to have many tactful conversations about "vested self-interest" being a nonstarter for the process. Everyone needed to consider the good of the whole, not just their little piece of the pie. This meant that strong personalities had to be both encouraged and kept in check. That was not easy, because there were many polarizing differences with people pulling in different directions. This was yet another reason to enlist good leaders who knew how to facilitate the process to yield productive results. They had to help people stand back and not get too personally invested in the result. They coached to focus on the solutions, not the problems. They needed to be persuaded to **hold the vision and trust the process.**

The last major hurdle (not chronologically, but logistically) related to a **nonaligned vision for the project.** Throughout the effort, people advocating for some legacy systems continued to create challenges because they tried to insist that certain elements from those systems be included—even if they did not score high on the matrix created to evaluate various features. Even when they weren't arguing about legacy systems, there were competing priorities for different stakeholders. Clients needed certain things, admin people had specific needs, line management needed other things, franchisees had their own requirements, country managers had broader specifications, and, of course, the global office had its own set of priorities. With at least six levels of stakeholders representing dozens of countries, all coming to the table with different levels of experiences, **the complexity was both fascinating and staggering at the same time.**

Getting organizational alignment with the vision wasn't just important—it was critical. Richard knew that **if all the people in an organization row in the same direction, that organization can dominate any industry, in any market, against any competition, at any time.** The key to the project's success was to implement that shared vision. He just had to get them all rowing in the same direction.

One of the final benefits of the co-creative process that Richard understood was the power of **shared resources**—which goes back to the concept of the wisdom of the crowd. In co-creation, the participants are not just sharing their knowledge; they are sharing their resources as well. Richard later learned that this continues to happen even after the original vision is realized.

After the debacle of the previous release, the co-created platform was ready to be rolled out. Weekly webinars continued, and regular emails were dramatically ramped up. Most important, an outside training and support company was brought in to train all the end users on the new platform as soon as it was implemented in their territories. One of the most salient points made by a team member during this time was that "most of the noise that people will express is that they don't know how to use something. It won't be that a feature doesn't exist or doesn't work."

Richard realized she was completely correct in her assessment. Thanks to the co-creative process, the most important functions were included in the platform, and they worked. Now people just needed to be trained to use it so the pushback against the platform could be minimized.

It was three years since the ad hoc committee first met and it was time to release the platform...again. What a difference the past year had made. This time, the company had used a co-creative process to complete the project and launch it. There had been strong leadership, almost total transparency, and exhaustive communication at all levels of the organization. Richard had realized during this journey that **in the co-creative process you give up control but gain engagement.**

The swarm of angry Goliath Beetles that had plagued the prior release were nonexistent this time. Oh, there were bugs—but they were manageable. There was pushback, but it was reasonable. There were problems, but they were not insurmountable. **Finally, after several years, co-creation achieved what competition and cooperation could not.** It produced a single organizational platform that was acceptable to almost everyone. It wasn't perfect—but it would serve as a foundation for what came next. Most notably, it was created by the stakeholders and for the stakeholders. Not just some of them—but all of them.

Richard had learned that the one crucial factor woven into the very fabric of a successful co-creative process was strong leadership at many levels. But not just any kind of leader—a co-creative leader. Someone who understood the ins and outs of the co-creative process. Leaders needed to be diplomatic gatekeepers. They could set expectations and allow input. They would welcome dialogue and help people feel validated for their contributions. Most important, they understood the importance of holding the vision and not the obstacles in front of them.

Richard had an opportunity to debrief with one of the key leaders of the process and learned even more. This individual was one of the most important people in helping get the project over the finishing line. His name was Bob, and he shared a lot with Richard about the process.

Bob explained that **the project managers created a "barking dog list"** of the people who were most passionate about their individual ideas. They were often the most unhappy stakeholders. The team felt that these people needed to be brought into the process because they were the most vocal critics. If they were forced to sit on the sidelines, they would keep barking, but they wouldn't help find any solutions. They would, in fact, add to the team's obstacles.

Then Bob wrote a "Dunkirk letter" to all the global stakeholders, like Churchill's famous speech (yes, Bob was British..."We shall fight on the beaches..."). He spoke of the need to move forward and that it was time to draw a line in the sand. Co-creation was powerful, but at the same time, decisions that were not always popular with some stakeholders. **Sometimes people think they know the solution when they don't fully understand the problem.** Co-creative leadership involves coaching and guiding people along a path to achieve the overarching vision of the project—a task that was not lost on Bob.

By using data-driven analysis with an in-house statistician, the project's leadership was able to show that certain elements of the old legacy systems, which some were insisting on including in the new platform, wouldn't be used by most people. This helped quiet most of the passionate defenders of other legacy system elements. While many of them had strong opinions, it was always the vision that drove the process. **Most stakeholders were more concerned about making a difference than making a point.** Hence, to their credit, they often let go of the things they were clinging to when the data gave them a different perspective.

Bob also said that the leaders had to move the process along while still allowing room for debate and discussion. Part of leadership in co-creation is allowing the process its own flow while steering it in a way that keeps it on track. The leaders had to set boundaries, but those boundaries were wide, and everyone knew that the project board was the final arbiter on all issues relating to the program. This was important to Richard. He did not want the project board to be viewed as a management puppet and to be guilty of what he called "rubber stamp syndrome." It was important to allow decisions that he didn't necessarily agree with but that didn't jeopardize the project. That was very difficult for many people leading the process (including Richard). However, it was also a key part of the project's success. Many people were arguing because they disagreed about what was most important. This was good, because it gave them the space to look at what was important for the whole organization.

Richard realized that creating a diverse group gives you a balanced view. A good leader allows debate while ensuring that it doesn't get personal. You must give them space to create and hold that space for people to be heard. For example, it is important to call on people who are not speaking up on their own. Everyone needs to participate. It may not be pleasant feedback, but it's honest, and it will help you sort out any issues much faster.

The process needs dissent, but not at the cost of group harmony. Displeasure can be a positive emotion within the proper framework. **What you can't work with is apathy; that is a nonstarter for successful co-creation.** Natural tension between some stakeholders (such as marketing people versus tech people) can enrich the results. When done right, they can translate the issues they have for one another. Richard found that this process was an eye opener for many people.

The platform was years in the making. It started in the 1st Paradigm with confusion and conflict; transitioned to the 2nd Paradigm, where it created anxiety and anger; and landed in the 3rd Paradigm, which resulted in a successful project that is still thriving more than 10 years later.

From this process, Richard learned that **sometimes you have to slow down to go fast.** Co-creation forced him to hit the brakes and bring all parties together to create something as a unified team. Once his team was formed, the organization was off to the races.

Co-creation can be a force multiplier for an organization. It helped Richard successfully bring his company forward into the 21st century.

Conclusion

Richard did not fully understand the importance and the power of the 3rd Paradigm when he started his journey, but we do, and we think more and more people can be empowered to integrate this concept into their companies. Even though Richard struggled with regular conflict and felt the co-creative process was at times incredibly tedious—it worked. He needed that slow pace to find a solution for his organization that would catapult its growth. The co-creative process led Richard and his stakeholders to a workable solution that launched smoothly and led rapidly to remarkable results. After the launch, Richard's organization continued to use collaborative groups, and their first major co-creative project remains a cornerstone of the company.

We believe the 3rd Paradigm has incalculable potential to solve the world's most pressing problems. As Richard's case demonstrates—and as we mentioned in Chapter 4—co-creation can be deployed only for special projects, or an entire organization can predominantly function using the 3rd Paradigm. Both approaches can lead to transformative results.

Just imagine the problems we could solve if we all decided to embrace the 3rd Paradigm in our lives. The world would be a much better place to work and live in.

Wouldn't it be amazing if governments weren't so divisive, but rather worked together on problems rather than fighting over them? We are suggesting the radical idea that we can solve political problems by co-creating, not combating. No longer would governments be the poster child for the 1st Paradigm.

Much like a conductor of an orchestra, Richard got everyone playing the same tune at the same time. Even if he had to step away for a moment, the show would have continued until he returned. That is the beauty of co-creation.

Yes, there is a leader, but one who builds consensus, maintains engagement, and holds the vision, rather than one who issues orders.

Just imagine the problems we could solve if we all decided to embrace the 3rd Paradigm in our lives. The world would be a much better place to work and live in.

CHAPTER 10

An Interview with the Authors

We gave great consideration to how we wanted to wrap up this unique work. We felt that the book was uncommon in several ways. **The concept of the 3rd Paradigm itself is an emerging idea that will have a growing impact on the way the world interacts and creates.** It shows the evolution from mere cooperation to the emergence of co-creation to achieve organizational goals. Crowdsourcing is one of the best examples of how this concept will become increasingly important. In addition, the book used data from a survey of thousands of people, interviews with many experts, research from scholars, the coauthors' personal experiences, and a case study interwoven throughout every chapter. This combination has led to a work that we believe will help shape the concept of co-creation in the future. We felt that this final chapter, laid out as an interview of the three authors, would be a helpful addition to the various elements we have already featured in this book.

Below is the interview, conducted by our publisher, Entrepreneur Books. We hope that you find our answers useful to your co-creative journey.

Entrepreneur: *We appreciate the opportunity to get this concept and this book into the world. Ivan, this is your fifth book published with Entrepreneur. Why did you select Entrepreneur to publish this work?*

Ivan: I have always enjoyed working with Entrepreneur. I've been writing for the online platform for more than 20 years. I feel that it is a great publishing house to bring forth ideas that are core to running a business, as well as ideas that are cutting-edge and evolving. Your ability to produce books, a printed magazine, and of course the wealth of online content makes it perfect to get these ideas out into the world, and that is our goal. We want to transform the way business operates in the world.

What inspired you to write this book?

Dawa: When Ivan and I first started talking about the idea for this book, I was involved in several major co-creative projects and experienced both the benefits and challenges of working co-creatively first-hand. These are challenging times for a lot of people, and the approaches of the 1st and 2nd Paradigms of competition and cooperation, while proven to yield certain outcomes, simply do not solve many of the major challenges that we are currently facing and that require new, innovative, and disruptive solutions, whether in the United States or around the world.

The concept of the 3rd Paradigm itself is an emerging idea that will have a growing impact on the way the world interacts and creates.

I work in the world of hypergrowth technology startups, where every day we are questioning the status quo and pushing ourselves to face and address some of the world's pressing problems, like climate change, the energy transition, the global financial system, risks of artificial intelligence, the threat of pandemics, the threat of wars, and the need for greater diversity, equity, and inclusion across our society and all sectors. Co-creation is still a limited or missing skill set for many leaders in this world, so we thought we would tackle the topic head-on.

Ivan: I experienced firsthand the three paradigms while running my global organization. I knew early on in my career that the Competition Paradigm led, at best, to a win-lose outcome. At worst, everyone lost under that paradigm. Cooperation was the paradigm that I trained under in graduate school. The idea of people working together as a team to solve problems was more effective and certainly provided a better work environment. However, during my career I saw that something was missing from this approach. There needed to be more buy-in on really challenging problems in the organization. **I discovered that the stakeholders were an incredible resource to co-create a solution to challenging problems.** In 1986, I formed my first co-creative body in my company (BNI). This group was called the "board of advisors," but the truth is they were more than advisors. I gave them almost complete authority to design, redesign, eliminate, or create new organizational policies that directly related to the clients (aka members) of the organization. It was crowdsourcing before the internet. It was a game changer for my company. Without them, I could not have scaled BNI into a global enterprise with more than 11,000 groups across the globe.

How have you engaged in co-creation?

Heidi: As a writer and editor, I've learned that book writing is almost always a co-creative process because many people are involved. Take this book, for example. We had more than 4,000 people contribute to it by responding to our survey. That is above and beyond the work of the authors and publishing team. By offering their perspectives, **the survey respondents contributed immensely to creating this book.**

Ivan: Soon after BNI's board of advisors, my management team and I began creating various co-creative bodies within the organization. Today there are a dozen well-established groups that address accountability benchmarks, strategic vision, tactical issues, technology, special events, and more.

Dawa: As a business and community leader, I have discovered that co-creation is at the heart of strong, values-driven, and highly entrepreneurial business cultures and communities. Today, my company is involved in several entrepreneurial and philanthropic undertakings that are powered by a co-creative approach. We have also focused specifically on following a co-creative process to writing this book, which we believe will further expose the reader to the diversity of ideas and solutions generated by a co-creative process.

Tell me about Richard's story. How closely aligned to a real story is it?

Heidi: The story has been anonymized, but everything in it happened to one of the co-authors.

Dawa: The story is real, all right. We wanted to pull back the curtain and give our readers a feeling for what it can be like to go through an important co-creative process inside a growing company facing major challenges. If you do some research on us, it won't be too hard to find out who the story is modeled after.

The book focuses on co-creation for all businesses. What extra considerations might need to be taken in environments or models other than business?

Ivan: Wouldn't the world be a truly amazing place if people focused on solutions and not problems? Wouldn't it be amazing if people could disagree without being totally disagreeable. Wouldn't it be incredible if we could create together rather than tear things down? That's what co-creation is all about. It gets people together for the singular purpose of holding a vision and not obsessing about the obstacles. It is possible to do these things. I've seen it, and I've been a party to it. We must start by having the desire and the will to do so. Then we can use this book to actually make it happen. **My greatest desire is for business to introduce this process to the world. Then maybe governments and bureaucracies might start to co-create solutions to the world's problems as well.**

My greatest desire is for business to introduce this process to the world. Then maybe governments and bureaucracies might start to co-create solutions to the world's problems as well.

Heidi: Getting direct stakeholder insight is crucial, whether the organization is a business, community group, or government. The only difference is the identity of the stakeholder.

When considering co-creation in a government setting, I would make sure the leaders of the process are realistic about the project timeline.

Governments might need to do things like hold public hearings or information sessions and secure taxpayer funding, which can potentially make the co-creative process much slower than if an individual business decided to address the same project.

Dawa: Institutions like governments are traditionally slow to change and adapt, yet they represent a great many people and their needs. Many representative voting systems are outdated and do not allow the public to take an active part in discussing and deciding on pressing issues, even though technology allows us to distribute and gather information with the click of a button, much faster and more efficiently than when those systems were created.

We are on the precipice of further acceleration of the co-creative opportunity across all sectors, as we have today the ability to reach directly into the hands, hearts, and minds of billions of people through their high-tech devices. Billions of people own smartphones, which encourages active contribution from many, many more people in the co-creative process that is society. In theory, every institution has the power to be in direct contact with their most important stakeholders around the clock. Some are conscious of this opportunity; others are not. When we see world events being influenced by social media, governments toppled, wars won or lost, and new global systems created faster and more efficiently and effectively than ever before, we are witnessing the power of co-creation happening right in front of our eyes. This power can be harnessed by anyone.

Our research clearly pointed to the need for better-trained leaders who know what to do, say, and model during each phase of the co-creative process.

How did the research findings of your survey challenge or support your notions of co-creation?

Ivan: I know that leadership is the key to the success of any enterprise. However, I was shocked at how that topic came up over and over and over again, relating to virtually every positive and negative element of the process. I am now convinced that it takes special leadership skills to accomplish co-creation within an organization. What I'm most proud of is that this text is a guidebook for how a leader can employ this through-out their organization.

Dawa: Co-creation is an imperfect process engaged in by imperfect people. Our study confirmed that there are several clear benefits and repeated challenges when following a co-creative process. How this is implemented and stewarded inside organizations really depends on the clarity leaders have about co-creation and their ability to inspire and maintain high levels of engagement among key participants. Many leaders try to wing it and engage in co-creative processes without strong frameworks or any understanding of what we covered in this book—and are surprised when their efforts backfire or fail. **Our research clearly pointed to the need for better-trained leaders who know what to do, say, and model during each phase of the co-creative process.** That is why we wrote this book.

Heidi: The importance of leadership emerged as a key theme from our survey respondents, even though the survey didn't specifically ask about leadership. Respondents wrote about the benefits of good leadership and the pitfalls of bad leadership nearly 2,000 times in the survey! Going into this project, I assumed leadership was important, but **the survey results reinforced just how important leadership is.**

How does co-creation work across cultures? Are there limitations or extra considerations that need to be accounted for outside the United States?

Dawa: By definition, cultures are often exclusive to some, and therefore inclusive to others. Values, perceptions, acceptable emotional responses, and behaviors can vary greatly across cultures and can have a strong impact on the success of co-creation. In addition, many of today's businesses are staffed by a remote and increasingly global workforce, which can add to and reinforce cultural differences. **It is important to do your homework and understand the value system and cultural context in which you operate, but we have designed our model to be culturally agnostic.**

Heidi: Cross-cultural awareness is crucial, especially if the co-creative team is dispersed. For instance, notions of communication and even time vary depending on the cultural context. What is effective and clear in one culture might be considered rude and out of touch in another. **Crosscultural co-creative teams could benefit from cultural awareness training, which can proactively address any communication issues that might otherwise arise.**

Ivan: Cultural differences are almost always a factor in doing business around the world. Interestingly, there is a culture that many of us don't perceive until we are immersed in a conversation about cultural differences: the culture of business and entrepreneurism. Businesspeople want to do things more efficiently and effectively. If we can offer an idea that enables them to do that, they will employ it in their operations in a way that is culturally relevant. The key is to not force a change on the culture but instead to offer a system or process that can be overlaid on the cultural context.

What have you learned about generational differences from your research?

Ivan: There were clearly some generational differences in people's view of co-creation. Despite those, I think co-creation can transcend those differing perspectives. In particular, I believe the younger generation is far better equipped and emotionally prepared to embrace co-creation in ways that older generations cannot and in some cases will not do. The next generation understands how to implement this strategy better because they literally grew up with the concept of crowdsourcing.

Dawa: Generational differences show that we are creatures of habit. **Co-creation is uncomfortable but highly valuable, so those who tend to do best with this approach are those willing to trade comfort for progress.** Those are often the younger generations. But today's economic landscape and fast-changing world

Co-creation is uncomfortable but highly valuable, so those who tend to do best with this approach are those willing to trade comfort for progress.

are leveling the playing field. All generations are exposed and experiencing the accelerated rate of change. Today's workforce consists of five generations working side by side, so resistance to co-creation is a luxury many people can't afford.

Heidi: The survey revealed nuances between generations and their views of co-creation in terms of advantages and disadvantages. Some differences were subtle, while others were not. If you're on a co-creative team, I would review these findings again. Also, keep in mind that most people support co-creation, but those who don't are likely to be of the baby boomer generation. You'll need to navigate the co-creation process while keeping these considerations in mind.

How can or does co-creation shape successful entrepreneurship?

Dawa: In many industries it has become best practice to operate leaner and closer to the customer and other stakeholders when creating products and services, shaping the value proposition, and building the company. This can lead to fewer products and services being launched that have no customer demand, which just wastes the company's and investors' time and money. Co-creation also tends to express less as just a strategy and more as an actual culture, and a culture of co-creation can be highly resilient, as more stakeholders have a sense of ownership, impact, and belonging. As Peter Drucker used to say, "Culture eats strategy for breakfast."

By bringing in stakeholders to solve a problem or improve a process, small-business owners can engage in co-creation and give their business a competitive edge.

Heidi: Especially for small businesses where the owner wears numerous hats, co-creation can help distribute the intellectual demands for innovation and process improvement. **By bringing in stakeholders to solve a problem or improve a process, small-business owners can engage in co-creation and give their business a competitive edge.**

Ivan: We opened this book by saying that "we live in an age of sweeping conflict, widespread skepticism, and intense anxiety." That is true today. I don't believe it is a statement of where we must go. I believe that **"What's in the way, becomes the way." Conflict, skepticism, and anxiety can be the motivation to find a different way to communicate and create a better world.** Co-creation can be that catalyst.

What are some challenges that are particularly well-suited for co-creation?

Dawa: Pressing global challenges that cannot be solved by one group or one country alone; pressing local issues that consume endless partisan debate without any practical breakthroughs; developing greater diversity, equity, and inclusion across the board; achieving better market fit for products faster and in a more cost-efficient way; and scaling businesses internationally.

Heidi: I'll answer that question by flipping it to share what I think isn't ripe for co-creation: personal development. I think anything that is uniquely personal in nature—What are my values? What legacy do I want to leave? Where do I want to take my career? What problem do I want to solve?—primarily requires self-reflection. Nearly anything else is suitable for co-creation, from micro-community projects to securing reliable internet to countries facing conflict.

Ivan: Co-creation is perfectly suited to projects that are highly complex and involve many people who bring various perspectives to the project. Involving people from various areas of the organization does create a natural tension; however, when done effectively, it also ensures that all voices are heard.

In what ways do you envision co-creation transforming society in the next 20 years?

Ivan: The most obvious area where co-creation can transform society is the integration of technology platforms and systems into the co-creative process. That said, the most important part to transform is the hearts and minds of leaders and stakeholders. **When knowledgeable leaders deploy an effective co-creative process in their organization, it will**

transform that organization. When enough organizations do it, it will transform the world.

Dawa: Paradigm shifts tend to unleash efficiencies and effectiveness above and beyond any prior thinking. As such, co-creation has become a tool by which businesses and organizations can leapfrog from old-world thinking and create new and better solutions that are more valuable and meaningful for all stakeholders. Technology is driving this change. From blockchain to open source AI, from co-creating entire value chains globally to reinventing how wars are fought and peace is kept. Co-creation is the key to help bring society into the 21st century.

Heidi: I suspect co-creation will transform society in ways I can't even imagine right now, with advances in technology paving the way. Not long ago, it was the work of sci-fi to think that we could communicate with someone and see them across distances; now it's hard to imagine life without videoconferencing. Large medical device projects might have more than 100 people involved in co-creating lifesaving treatments and equipment. Some surgeries can now be done remotely. It's exciting to think about what will come next through co-creation!

How will the advancements in Artificial Intelligence alter the opensource landscape and how will that add to the process of co-creation?

Ivan: Artificial intelligence (AI) has already begun to transform numerous aspects of our lives, and the world of open source software is no exception. As AI technology continues to evolve, it is likely to have a significant impact on the open source landscape and the process of co-creation.

One of the most significant ways in which AI is likely to alter the open source landscape is through the use of machine learning (ML) algorithms. ML algorithms enable machines to learn and improve their performance over time, without being explicitly programmed to do so. This has numerous implications for open source software, as ML algorithms can be used to automate repetitive tasks and enhance the accuracy and efficiency of software development.

For example, ML algorithms can be used to identify patterns in code and detect bugs, enabling developers to quickly and efficiently identify and fix issues. ML algorithms can also be used to suggest improvements to code or automate the process of testing and deployment, reducing the amount of time and effort required for these tasks.

Another way in which AI is likely to impact the open source landscape is through the development of new tools and frameworks. As AI technology continues to evolve, we can expect to see new AI-powered tools and frameworks that are specifically designed for open source development. These tools may include AI-powered code editors, automated code reviews, and even AI-generated code snippets.

These tools will add a new layer to the process of co-creation, enabling developers to work together more efficiently and effectively. AI-powered tools can automate tedious tasks, freeing up developers to focus on more complex and creative aspects of software development. They can also improve the quality of code by detecting and fixing errors, ensuring that the software is more stable and reliable.

Perhaps one of the most exciting aspects of AI in the context of open source software is the potential for AI to facilitate more diverse and inclusive co-creation. AI algorithms can be used to analyze code contributions and identify patterns in the ways in which different contributors work. This can help to identify biases and disparities in the contributions of different groups, enabling project leaders to take steps to address these issues and create a more inclusive environment.

Furthermore, AI algorithms can be used to facilitate communication and collaboration between contributors, even when they are working in different time zones or using different languages. This can help to overcome language and cultural barriers, enabling a more diverse group of people to participate in open source development.

AI is likely to have a significant impact on the open source landscape and the process of co-creation. Through the use of machine learning algorithms and the development of new AI-powered tools and frameworks, AI will enable developers to work together more efficiently and effectively. It will also help to create a more diverse and inclusive environment for open source development, by identifying and addressing biases and disparities in the contributions of different groups. As AI technology continues to evolve, we can expect to see even more exciting innovations in the world of open source software development.

Heidi: I believe the advancements in AI have the potential to greatly alter the way we work, similar to how the advent of the desktop computer profoundly changed our daily lives. In the business world, who isn't tied to their computers for work? Very few of us.

I suspect AI will be integrated into the world in incalculable ways, leaving fallout behind it. Jobs will be lost; jobs will be gained.

The process of co-creation will be affected for reasons as Ivan gave, and I think the role of AI will also underscore the importance of actual human interaction. Some of the tasks that we might have done together will be aided by, if not completely done, by AI. Yet, the fundamental need for human interaction will remain. The isolation forced by quarantining during the pandemic taught us that. And who isn't relieved when a real person answers the phone if they call a business or healthcare facility rather than an automated assistant? Almost everyone.

I suspect AI could be like the best colleague: doing a great job with its assigned tasks, thereby enabling everyone else to focus on what they do best, too. This can undoubtedly aid any co-creative process.

With the advancements in AI, however, I also believe we need to remember the phrase 'with great power comes great responsibility.' This might be an advancement that is more significant than the printing press, the mass commercialization of electricity, and the industrial revolution. It's too early to tell, but I do believe we need to steer this ship carefully.

If readers leave with only one message about co-creation, what do you want them to know?

Dawa: There is easy, and then there is good. Co-creation is not easy, but it can be very good for solving the right kind of problem with the right group of people at the right time. **It is a transformative practice that involves letting go of egos, grasping, and fixation to make real space**

for other people's input. And it requires sustained attention, aware-ness, and focus to convert that input into successful execution. As we mentioned earlier in Chapter 2, a popular proverb says, "If you want to go fast, go alone; if you want to go far, go together."

Heidi: Co-creation might feel messy, but it is achievable and worth the effort. Co-creation can help solve some of the world's most pressing problems—and those problems can be tackled by individuals and busi-nesses, not only governments.

Ivan: I agree with Heidi: It does feel messy, complex, and often frustrat-ing. As we said in Chapter 9, "Co-creation is a thing of beauty and a muddy mess. It holds two places in reality at the same time." **It takes a special type of leader (or leaders, to be exact) to have the patience and vision to effectively implement the concept.** Our goal with this book was to give those leaders the foundational concepts and tools they need to do just that.

How do you recommend people get started?

Dawa: The key to co-creation is involving other people. Our book pro-vides a practical model and sequential process anyone can use to achieve results with co-creation, but the first thing is to talk to the people you want to engage in the process. The emphasis in co-creation is on "co." So open up about your plans and start to include important stakehold-ers in your considerations. That is the biggest shift and most important transformation. You have to begin to see other people not as part of the problem but as a critical part of the solution. If you want, share this book with everyone you want to work with so you have a common model to work from. It is always easier to find your way through new terrain if more than one person is looking at the map. This book is that map.

Heidi: Identify the problem you want to solve, and then use the Co-Creation Model we presented in the book to get started. The clock's ticking!

Ivan: There is a proverb that says: "When is the best time to plant an oak tree? Answer: 20 years ago. When is the second best time? Answer: today." You have already started this journey by reading this book. Now start finding ways to implement co-creation within your organization. It won't be easy. Most great things are difficult to achieve. If you look for excuses, you'll find them. But if you look for solutions, you'll find those instead. **Start today and hold the vision not the obstacles.**

Index

About the Authors

Dr. Ivan Misner is the Founder & Chief Visionary Officer of BNI, the world's largest business networking organization. Founded in 1985, BNI now has more than 11,000 chapters, located throughout every populated continent of the world. Each year, BNI members pass millions of referrals, generating billions of U.S. dollars in business each year.

Dr. Misner earned his Ph.D. from the University of Southern California. He is a *New York Times* bestselling author who has written more than 28 books, including the recent *Who's in Your Room? The Question That Will Change Your Life.* He is the recipient of the John C. Maxwell Transformational Leadership Award and is also a columnist for Entrepreneur.com. He has been a university professor and a member of the board of trustees for the University of La Verne. In addition, he has been featured in the *Los Angeles Times, The Wall Street Journal,* and *The New York Times* and made frequent appearances on TV and radio, including CNN, the BBC, and *Today* on NBC.

Dawa Tarchin Phillips is the founder and CEO of Empowerment Holdings, an international leadership development and coaching company working with innovative founders, CEOs and their teams. He is president of the International Mindfulness Teachers Association, a global professional organization for mindfulness teachers from 30 countries who teach in 13 languages.

Dawa completed two three-year meditation retreats and is a member of the prestigious Transformational Leadership Council and the Association of Transformational Leaders, a board member of the World Business Academy, and a leading voice in the global mindfulness movement. He is an investor, researcher and polymath, and contributing author of books, articles, and prolifically cited research papers on mindfulness, leadership, neuroscience, and Buddhism, and a Nautilus Book Award Gold Recipient. His work has been featured in *The New York Times*, Huffington Post, *Forbes*, and *Fast Company*.

Dr. Heidi Scott Giusto is a writer, editor, and communications consultant. She owns Career Path Writing Solutions, a consulting firm dedicated to helping people communicate when it matters most. Heidi earned her PhD in History from Duke University and her master's and undergraduate degrees from Youngstown State University. She has taught at numerous leading universities. Heidi collaborates with clients from diverse professional backgrounds and specializes in business, leadership, and self-help books.

BNI

BNI, the world's largest business networking organization, was founded by Dr. Ivan Misner in 1985 as a way for businesspeople to generate referrals in a structured, professional environment. The organization has thousands of chapters with hundreds of thousands of members on every populated continent. Since its inception, BNI members have passed millions of referrals and generated billions of dollars in business for its participants.

The primary purpose of the organization is to pass qualified business referrals to its members. BNI's philosophy can be summed up in two simple words: Givers Gain®. If you give business to people, you will get business from them. BNI allows only one person per profession to join a chapter. The program is designed to help members develop long-term relationships, creating a basis for trust and, inevitably, referrals. The mission of BNI is to help members increase their business through a structured, positive, and professional word-of-mouth program that enables them to develop long-term, meaningful relationships with quality business professionals.

To find a chapter near you, contact BNI; you can visit its website at https://www.bni.com/.

EMPOWERMENT
HOLDINGS
INTELLIGENT LEADERSHIP AND QUALITY OF LIFE IN BUSINESS

Empowerment Holdings was founded by Dawa Tarchin Phillips in 2007—during the height of the global financial crises—to support the growing number of leaders worldwide seeking more intelligent and wise leadership practices and quality of life. The company's mission is to help leaders and professionals in corporate environments around the world lead their lives with greater integrity, clarity, purpose and passion. It does so through proprietary, scalable and digitally-enabled processes to achieve consistent, long term behavior change, and personal and professional growth.

Printed in the USA
CPSIA information can be obtained
at www.ICGtesting.com
LVHW022213100923
757571LV00001B/1